Katie Souza's book *The S*[...] "[...]
loaded" with valuable revelation and life-transforming
insight regarding deliverance from demonic assaults on
the body, soul, family, finances, and every aspect of life. I
found it to also be refreshingly practical, as it offers easy
activation and application for the reader. Katie, like Jesus,
longs to see captives set free. She has committed her life
and ministry to pursuing freedom, healing, and deliverance for those who are bound, oppressed, and tormented.
This book is focused on the truth found in Christ and
His Word that will set you free. Read, apply, and enjoy
new realms of freedom and liberty in Christ.

—PATRICIA KING
AUTHOR, MINISTER, MEDIA HOST
WWW.PATRICIAKING.COM

In her groundbreaking book *The Serpent and the Soul*,
Katie Souza, my dear friend and coauthor of our book,
Idols Riot!, has just single-handedly propelled the ministry
of deliverance into another dimension of breakthrough.
Her revelatory teaching examines and traces the relationship between the condition of our souls and the activities
of insidious spirit entities that Jesus called "serpents" in
the Great Commission in the Gospel of Mark.

Katie Souza sheds light on a very important part of
the Great Commission that until now has remained, for
the most part, a mystery. Have you ever wondered what
Jesus meant when He said, "These signs will follow those
who believe: In My name they will cast out demons; they
will speak with new tongues; they will *take up serpents*"
(Mark 16:17–18, NKJV, emphasis added)? Laying hands on
the sick and casting out demons seem self-explanatory in
the tone of the Great Commission, but what does it mean
to "take up serpents"?

In this blockbuster book, Katie Souza breaks the pro-
verbial veil of mystery behind the expression "take up serpents." She will show you that much of our spiritual ills

are directly connected to these spirit creatures known as serpents. She will show you that just as there are different types of serpents in the natural, so it is in the spiritual realm. Commonly known players in this space of serpents are demonic entities such as Leviathan and Python, which have a destructive impact on the souls and destinies of mankind.

Katie Souza unveils strategic spiritual tools that believers can use to assert their Christ-given dominion over all of these demons, and she shows how we can set ourselves free from their idolatrous pantheons. I highly recommend this book for all ministers of the gospel and saints alike.

—DR. FRANCIS MYLES
BEST-SELLING AUTHOR, *I SPEAK TO THE EARTH* AND
THE ORDER OF MELCHIZEDEK

The
Serpent
and the
Soul

The
Serpent
and the
Soul

Katie Souza

CHARISMA HOUSE

control over and do not assume any responsibility for third-party websites or their content.

For more resources like this, visit MyCharismaShop.com and the author's website at katiesouza.com.

Cataloging-in-Publication Data is on file with the Library of Congress.
International Standard Book Number: 978-1-63641-389-1
E-book ISBN: 978-1-63641-390-7

1 2024
Printed in the United States of America

Most Charisma Media products are available at special quantity discounts for bulk purchase for sales promotions, premiums, fund-raising, and educational needs. For details, call us at (407) 333-0600 or visit our website at www.charismamedia.com.

This book is dedicated to the original snake hunter, Jesus Christ, the Seed of the woman who crushed the head of the serpent—once for all.

CONTENTS

Foreword by Duane "Dog the Bounty Hunter" Chapman . . . xiii

Chapter 1   Take Up Serpents 1

Chapter 2   The Religious Spirit and Idols 11

Chapter 3   Snakes Hate Fire 31

Chapter 4   The Antivenom Power of Jesus 49

Chapter 5   Shaking Off Venomous Vipers
Through Communion 73

Chapter 6   Leviathan: The King of the Children
of Pride 97

Chapter 7   Trauma, Leviathan, and Witchcraft 117

Chapter 8   Python Squeezes Out Your Gains 139

Chapter 9   Healing and Deliverance From Idols 163

Chapter 10   Fertility and Food .187

Chapter 11   Commissioned to Be a Snake Hunter 211

Notes 229

About the Author 235

FOREWORD

By Duane "Dog the Bounty Hunter" Chapman

My sister Katie Souza has been a big part of our lives for some years now. She and my wife, Francie, are best friends, and I call her my sister because that's how close we have become during this time. We're like family—so close that Sister Katie officiated at my wedding to Francie, and then we all moved together to Florida so we could do ministry. We even lived on Sister Katie and her husband's property until Francie and I found our own perfect place.

Just a fast, fun story: while we were there, I had a seven-foot pet alligator named Wally that lived in Sister Katie's pond. One day I freaked her out when she came out to the pool and saw me by the bank of the pond, lifting Wally's tail and petting the entire length of its underside. That and many other animal tales have earned me the nicknames "Noah Dog" and "Dr. Doolittle Dog" among our inner circle of friends.

Sister Katie, Francie, and I now minister together in prisons all around the United States. It's in these meetings that I've gotten to see what my sister Katie is really made of in the Holy Ghost. And ministering with Francie and my sister Katie has really brought out the Holy Ghost in me and the call God put on my life when I was a kid.

I was raised in the Assemblies of God, saved at a young age, baptized in the Holy Ghost at church camp at age seven or eight, and received many powerful prophecies that I was called to the ministry. But as an adult I joined the Devils Disciples, which was a sister club to the Hell's Angels, and in the seventies found myself in prison for first-degree murder. I didn't pull the trigger; I didn't even see the shooting. I only heard the shot, and I knew it was an accident. But in the seventies in Texas, if you didn't call the police, you were just as guilty as if you pulled the trigger. So a jury convicted five of us for that crime, and I was sentenced to five years and a day in a Texas state penitentiary.

While I was in prison, the Lord really showed me a lot of favor. I became the warden's barber and the inmate counselor. But while I was incarcerated, I also got my first confirmation that I would eventually become a bounty hunter. I had a friend whose mama died while we were inside. The day of her passing, out of his grief, my friend decided to make a run for it and escape the prison walls to go to her funeral. I knew the guards in the towers were well armed and wouldn't think twice about gunning him down. So I chased after him, tackling him to the ground to save his life. That's when an officer came up behind me and, throwing a pair of handcuffs on the ground, said, "Hook him up, Bounty Hunter."

After prison I became Dog the Bounty Hunter and since have arrested over ten thousand offenders in my forty-year career. I thought my forte as a bounty hunter was beating people up and throwing them in jail. However, when my bounty hunting was featured on a reality show, the part of the program everyone liked best was what they called "the backseat ride." After hunting down my suspects and roughing them up, I would put them in the backseat of the car, give them a cigarette, and then pour Jesus down their throat. Nobody ever said no to either the cigarette or, more importantly, the Lord. To this day I run into people I have previously arrested, in airports and restaurants all around the country, who say their lives were totally changed the day of their backseat ride.

Now, because I grew up in the Assemblies of God, I've been in meetings with healing evangelists like Oral Roberts, Kathryn Kuhlman, and Betty Baxter. I've seen miracles that were incredible: goiters popping off necks, wheelchairs and crutches being piled up because they were no longer needed. But I have never seen miracles like the ones I've witnessed while visiting prisons with my sister Katie.

At one recent event it seemed like every four feet I walked, demons were being cast out. People were yelling, spitting, throwing up, and receiving wild miracles! At all our events cancer tumors disappear, toxins ooze out of people's bodies, crooked spines totally straighten, people get out of wheelchairs, and hundreds have metal rods, plates, screws, and bolts disappear from their bodies. One girl even had a razor blade she had swallowed to try to kill herself completely dissolve. God is amazing, and He does amazing things when my sister Katie ministers. I've seen many of these miracles with my own eyes—in and out of meetings.

Once, Francie was hanging out with Sister Katie, and Francie fell and broke her ankle. It was so bad the bone was sticking out sideways under her skin, and when Francie saw it, she just knew she would need surgery. All the way to the hospital, Sister Katie was praying in the Spirit, speaking over the bones, saying, "God, I've seen You move bones hundreds of times; now I need·You to do this for my best friend." And she did not let up.

When I arrived at the hospital, Francie had gone into shock. Her ankle was covered with a blanket, and Sister Katie was sitting at the foot of the hospital bed with her hands on Francie's ankle. Then I saw Sister Katie's shoulders go back like she was gearing up for a fight. She shook herself and cracked her neck, and it was on like Donkey Kong. We all started praying fiercely in that room—I was praying in tongues; Francie was praying in tongues. Sister

Katie was praying in tongues and in English, asking her angel to move Francie's bone and then for the Holy Spirit to regrow the bone matter so everything would stay in its proper place.

After praying for about fifteen minutes, Sister Katie pulled the blanket back and yelled, "It's working! It's working!" The bone had moved back in place, and the swelling was almost all the way gone. The next day she was walking practically pain-free, and her ankle had just a tiny bit of swelling. Francie was so healed that we all went to the beach that weekend, and Francie even carried a heavy cooler full of food across a long stretch of sand.

God even healed me through my sister. Once while we were doing a meeting together, I had pulled a muscle, and though I rarely ask for prayer, I thought, "I'm going to interrupt my sister in the middle of her preaching and have her pray for me." So I stopped the meeting in front of the entire crowd to have my sister Katie pray. I went home that night, got in bed, and when I woke up, I realized I was healed!

Yet even though we have seen hundreds of miracles, the most outstanding miracle moments are when souls are saved—and thousands have come to Christ at the meetings that my sister Katie, Francie, and I lead together.

In this book my sister will show you how to pray for yourself and other people in the same way I have seen her pray for hundreds of others. She shares the same kinds of prayers she said when all those miracles I've seen took place. You definitely won't be a wimpy Christian after reading *The Serpent and the Soul*. In fact the gates of hell will tremble and never prevail over you again! Read this book, and then read it again, and you will behold the power of God in your life!

CHAPTER 1

TAKE UP SERPENTS

Behold, I give you the authority to trample on serpents and scorpions, and over all the power of the enemy, and nothing shall by any means hurt you.
—LUKE 10:19, NKJV

SEVERAL YEARS AGO I had a remarkable encounter with a seasoned prophetic minister while I was speaking at an event led by Patricia King, another great prophetic minister. After the session, the three of us went out for dinner. Before our food arrived, the prophetic minister said, "While you were standing at the podium, I saw you in the spirit. You were covered from head to toe with scars—scars from all the battles you've endured—and beneath your feet were thousands of snakes that you had trampled."

Trust me when I say there has been a war for this revelation, and the result is that I have been mantled as a snake hunter in the spirit. I've faced down the powers of hell as they attempted to stop this insight from being made known to the body of Christ. You will see as you read and then act on the biblical truths in this book that the battle was worth every scar. Your life and authority are about to radically shift as you become a snake hunter too.

A woman once wrote to tell me she had stopped sending her monthly support to my ministry because she saw a swarm of black snakes dragging me down to the bottom of a healing pool to drown me. Little did she know that by ending her support, she was coming into agreement with the serpents' plan to take me out. Good luck with that.

The minister's vision exactly reflects what Jesus said in Luke 10:19: "Behold, I give you the authority to trample on serpents and scorpions, and over all the power of the enemy, and nothing shall by any means hurt you" (NKJV). When Jesus mentions having the authority to trample on serpents, is He solely referring to the body of Christ having power over snakes in the natural world?

We see an example of this in Acts 28. Paul had just endured a harrowing shipwreck and found himself on the island of Malta, collecting firewood to combat the cold. In his haste he unknowingly gathered a venomous viper among the sticks. When he tossed the bundle into the fire, the serpent, agitated by the heat, was driven out of the sticks and fastened itself on Paul's hand. Remarkably, Paul simply shook off the venomous viper and suffered no harm. This story exemplifies our authority over natural serpents.

Yet when we closely examine Luke 10:19 in the context of what Jesus was conveying, we can discern a much broader message. To grasp this fully, let's revisit the passage in the framework of the verses surrounding it.

First the Lord handpicked and dispatched seventy individuals, sending them out in pairs to places He intended to visit (v. 1). Then verse 17 says, "The seventy returned with joy, saying, 'Lord, even the demons are subject to us in Your name'" (NKJV). Here we see the disciples celebrating because they had been given authority over demons in Jesus' name. Upon hearing this, Jesus fortified their victory by saying He saw Satan, that old serpent, "fall like lightning from heaven" (v. 18, NKJV). It's after this that Jesus proclaims we have His authority to tread on serpents, scorpions, and all the enemy's power and remain unhurt in the process (v. 19).

Thus the context makes it clear that Jesus has given us total authority and power not just over snakes in the natural but also over demonic spirits that manifest in the guise of serpents. In fact I believe many of the demons the seventy disciples cast out during their mission trips were snakes.

One might think the notion of demons appearing in the form of snakes is outrageous. However, the very first encounter with a demonic entity recorded in the Bible was Satan assuming the form of a serpent in the garden. It was this snake that tempted Eve and Adam to partake of the forbidden fruit, leading to all humanity's fall. Even at the end of the Bible, in Revelation 12, Satan is referred to as "that old serpent" (v. 9, KJV). This continuity suggests that throughout biblical history, demons often adopt the serpent's guise.

Their objective? To "hurt" us, as emphasized in Luke 10:19. Let's take a closer look at the term *hurt* used in this scripture. The Greek word is *adikeō*, and it conveys the idea of to "(actively) do wrong (morally, socially or physically)."[1] Let's break this down.

First these demons are on a mission to inflict moral harm by luring you into sin. They'll tempt you to be bitter and unforgiving, to spend your money recklessly, to cheat and steal, to engage in sexual sin, to argue with your spouse, and to rebel against authority. These serpents will even drive you to eat excessively and consume the wrong foods, like the original serpent did in the garden. The list of the ways they manipulate you and the opportunities they present for you to err is vast. (We will dive into these in more detail throughout this book.) Their goal is to morally compromise you because if they succeed in making you sin, they gain a legal foothold to continue their destructive mission against you.

But the hurt doesn't stop at morality; it extends to social spheres as well. These serpents are relentless in their efforts to disrupt every aspect of your social life, be it with family members, friends, coworkers, or even your spouse. They weave their way into the fabric of your relationships, creating obstacles, strife, and seemingly insurmountable communication issues. If you've ever felt like your marriage is hitting a wall that you can't seem to overcome, it could very well be caused by serpentine activity. We will unpack this more in upcoming chapters.

These demonic serpents also weave themselves into the fabric of our society at the highest levels. In ancient Greece and Rome the leaders and the people worshipped the statues of many ancient gods. Snakes were often carved into these images, wrapped around the bodies of the gods or the staffs of power they clasped in their hands. Demonic serpents have been operating at the governmental level since ancient times, and their power is only increasing. It is horrific how many of our political officials are controlled by these spirits, as this enables Satan to release his agenda against the people of the nations through those leaders.

I remember an incident that happened during a recent presidential election. While leading prayer on Suzanne Hinn's National Prayer Call, I had a word from the Lord that a python spirit was squeezing out the conservative candidate's votes at the electronic ballot boxes. Over a thousand people joined with me to come against it. Not long after the call ended, national news media announced that election officials had discovered the electronic balloting system was taking the conservative candidate's votes and recording them for the opposing candidate. Busted.

Another facet of the term *hurt* includes these demons' actively causing you physical harm. Believe it or not, demonic serpents are the source of countless physical ailments. Whether it's arthritis, gout, eye and ear disorders, spinal issues, cancers, respiratory problems, or a host of other conditions, these malevolent entities can have a deadly impact on your physical health. More on that as we go.

MIRACLE TESTIMONY

During one of my teachings a woman named Pat was in the audience. She had a walnut-sized tumor in her breast that had become very uncomfortable—even painful. The doctors had diagnosed it as stage IV cancer. Remarkably, without any prior knowledge of her presence, I received a word of knowledge and declared, "Someone here is being healed of a breast tumor."

Pat immediately felt something leave her breast; then the tumor vanished. At the end of the session she came up to testify that she had been praying for seven days for the Lord to burn that cancer out. As she stood there attesting to the miracle, she continued, "I have to be very careful how I test it here, but I've been squishing myself every way I can in public without being inappropriate, and I can't feel a thing!"

What happened next was truly heartwarming. Pat is quite petite, standing at just four feet nine, while her husband is considerably taller. After she shared her testimony, he couldn't contain his excitement and rushed onto the stage to give her what they affectionately call their "signature hug." Throughout their entire marriage he would frequently pick her up and embrace her tightly, leaving her little legs dangling in the air.

When Pat was battling cancer, she and her husband couldn't do their signature hug because it was too painful for her. However, when he rushed to the platform and lifted her in the usual tight squeeze, something extraordinary happened. As he gently set her down, she looked up at him and exclaimed, "And it didn't even hurt!" Her husband burst into tears.

Pat later underwent a test, and the result was nothing short of miraculous—no more tumor, no more stage IV cancer. Praise be to God! (In a future chapter I will show you the biblical connection between serpents and cancer.)

These serpents are out to hurt our health in every way, yet the authority of the Lord Jesus Christ gives us the right to trample them!

WE ALL CAN "TAKE UP" SERPENTS

Jesus Himself declared that we can remove these serpents from both our and others' lives. His clear words concerning this are found in the Great Commission, specifically Mark 16:15–18. Let's examine it closely.

> And He said to them, "Go into all the world and preach the gospel to every creature. He who believes and is baptized will be saved; but he who does not believe will be condemned. And these signs will follow those who believe: In My name they will cast out demons; they will speak with new tongues; *they will take up serpents*; and if they drink anything deadly, it will by no means hurt them; they will lay hands on the sick, and they will recover."
> —MARK 16:15–18, NKJV, EMPHASIS ADDED

According to Jesus, all believers are entrusted with the responsibility to go forth and share the gospel. As they do, they will cast out demons, speak in new tongues, lay hands on the sick for their recovery, and, yes, *take up serpents*. What does this mean?

The Greek term for *take up* is *airō*, and it carries a profound meaning: "to remove" or "to take off or away what is attached to anything."[2] The implications of this are shocking. It indicates that these serpents can attach themselves to anything in your life—and that you are called to remove them. They can latch on to your marriage, your relationships, your family, your children, your physical body, your finances, your business, your government, and even your ministry, stifling your prosperity and growth. There's virtually nothing these serpents won't coil themselves around. Unfortunately this isn't an exaggeration; it's a harsh reality. Thank God we have been given authority to take them up from any place to which they have attached themselves.

It's curious how rarely this aspect of the Great Commission is expounded. Many ministers focus on preaching the gospel, baptizing, and healing the sick, but they omit the vital role of taking up serpents. Either these ministers associate it with churches that handle literal snakes in their services as a way of demonstrating their faith, or they skip over this topic and avoid operating in healing and deliverance because of fear or lack of knowledge. Taking up demonic serpent spirits is an aspect of spiritual warfare that hasn't been deeply explored, yet it's right there in the words of Jesus, who unequivocally says this is a sign that will follow believers as part of their divine mission.

It's crucial to dwell on this point: Jesus expects *every single believer*, not just the famous figures known for deliverance or healing, to be able to take up serpents. If you haven't removed a serpent from yourself, your friends, or even strangers, then you are not operating in the full authority Jesus gave us.

THE LEGAL LANDING STRIPS

Now let's delve into some of the reasons these serpents gain their legal right to attack us in the first place. Consider John 14:30, where Jesus says, "I will not talk with you much more, for the prince (evil genius, ruler) of the world is coming. And he has no claim on Me. [He has nothing in common with Me; there is nothing in Me that belongs to him, and he has no power over Me]."

I absolutely love this verse because Jesus unveils a key principle behind how many demonic spirits gain the legal right to afflict us. When we share something in common with them, they have a "claim" on us, which then gives them power to rule over our lives.

So, what might we possibly have in common with a demonic serpent? There are too many potential claims to list, but I will share some basics here, as well as more points throughout this book.

SIN BREAKS THE HEDGE

The first point to consider is sin. Sin is a gateway that can invite a serpent in that is seeking to hurt you. Ecclesiastes 10:8 says, "He who digs a pit [for others] will fall into it, and whoever breaks through a fence or a [stone] wall, a serpent will bite him."

This verse conveys a profound truth: God has set a protective hedge around you (Job 1:10), but you can inadvertently breach it through sin. It's crucial to grasp that when you sin, you break a hole in that protective hedge; then a serpent can slither in to inflict harm.

The Amplified Bible, Classic Edition emphasizes another aspect of this, challenging the person "who digs a pit [for others]." You can sin against yourself by engaging in behaviors like excessive drinking, drug use, or pornography, which will puncture God's protective hedge. However, you can also sin against others. Certain actions, such as adultery, not only harm you but also hurt your relationships with family members and others. This sin effectively breaks a hole in the hedge around you.

Also, when you gossip about others, judge and criticize them, or mentally, physically, or emotionally harm others in any way, you are digging a pit for them. This compromises your own hedge and allows a serpent to bite both you and the other people.

Through Christ's sacrifice we are no longer slaves to sin, and sin can't exert dominion over us. (See Romans 6.) Yet the horrible truth is that we still continually submit to its power. Believe it or not, we don't have to sin, as we are under the control of the Holy Spirit. We will be talking about this extensively in upcoming chapters. But for now we will continue to look at what happens when we don't believe we have power over sin.

SINS OF THE MOUTH

As indicated previously, if you use your mouth to speak words of evil and destruction against others, it can provide a legal landing strip for these slimy serpent assaults. Let's examine Romans 3:13–14, which shockingly states, "Their throat is a yawning grave; they use their tongues to deceive (to mislead and to deal treacherously). The venom of asps is beneath their lips. Their mouth is full of cursing and bitterness."

When you employ your tongue for deceit, misleading, or lying, or when your speech is characterized by cursing, complaining, and bitterness, you essentially harbor "the venom of asps...beneath {your} lips." When you speak about people or situations in a negative way, you are literally spitting snake venom at them, which could make both them and you sick!

It's essential to understand that bitterness is a major doorway to serpents. When we allow bitterness to fester—whether due to personal hurts, wounds, or insults from others—and we fail to forgive as instructed in the Bible, we inadvertently create a significant gateway for demonic serpentine forces. This includes speaking negatively about others, texting or gossiping about them, spreading rumors, or constantly dwelling on grievances.

Other translations of Romans 3:13 say, "Their throat is an open tomb" (NKJV) or "an open grave" (ESV). This underscores the profound truth that "death and life are in the power of the tongue," as stated in Proverbs 18:21. You possess the ability to speak life or death with your words. When you choose deceit, lies, bitterness, and cursing, you're not imparting life; you are unleashing death—through the form of a serpent strike.

Do you want to be complicit in allowing a snakelike attack on yourself, your family members, your finances, your life, or even someone else? You might think, "Well, that person deserves it." Yet in reality your actions are far worse than anything these individuals might have done to you, for you've effectively released a demonic serpent to assail them and perhaps even take them out. Believe me, when you harbor the venom of asps under your lips, the consequences of your words can be devastating, leading to sickness, disease, and a multitude of problems.

ACTIVATION

Let's move into an activation exercise. Have you been engaging in falsehoods and misleading with your words, as mentioned in Romans 3? Have you been cursing others, uttering malevolent words about them? Have you become embittered over a situation in your marriage or with family members, finding it impossible to cease your complaints, anger, and resentment? Is your mouth teeming with the venom of asps due to your cursing and bitterness?

Remember, Jesus provided you with power over sin! Right now I encourage you to ask the Holy Spirit to reveal areas where you need to seek the cleansing power of the blood of Jesus and where you must repent for using your words to malign others and harbor bitterness in your heart.

Let's take a moment to pray together. Please repeat after me:

> *Lord God, I do not want the venom of asps under my lips to taint my words, hurt others, and harm myself. I repent for every word of bitterness and cursing, and I ask that You wash every word with Jesus' blood to erase it from the court record forever. I understand that my words possess the power of life and death. I choose to speak life—into my family, my finances, and my future. I want to speak life, not death, over others.*
>
> *I also repent for using my words to deceive and lie. I repent for any negativity, complaints, and curses that have flowed from my mouth, causing me to spew venomous and deadly words at others or even myself and my family. Father, forgive me. Father, cleanse me. And, Jesus, remove this demonic assignment from my life through the power of Your cross. In Your name, amen.*

CHAPTER 2

THE RELIGIOUS SPIRIT AND IDOLS

*They spit venom like deadly snakes; they
are like cobras that refuse to listen.*
—PSALM 58:4, NLT

SINS RELATED TO a religious spirit are frequently connected to demonic serpents. Do you recall what both John the Baptist and Jesus called the Pharisees? Matthew 3:7 says, "But when he [John the Baptist] saw many of the Pharisees and Sadducees coming for baptism, he said to them, 'You brood of vipers, who warned you to flee from the wrath to come?'" (NASB).

By addressing these men as a "brood of vipers," John the Baptist was essentially indicating they were being controlled by demonic snakes. These individuals were consumed by a religious spirit, which gave serpents the right to manipulate and control them.

Jesus also used this phrase when speaking to the Pharisees. Matthew 23:33 reads, "You serpents, you brood of vipers, how are you to escape being sentenced to hell?" (ESV). Jesus didn't mince words. He even indicated they wouldn't escape the consequences of hell because of their religious attitudes and the demonic serpents they allowed to direct them.

Have you ever encountered exceptionally religious people? They can sometimes utter the harshest and most hurtful words. It can feel like you're being bitten by venomous snakes because, in a way, you are. They have the venom of asps under their tongues, and they are spitting that poisonous venom at you.

Spitting cobras are a type of poisonous snake. They not only inject venom when they bite, but they can also spit venom at possible threats. Similarly, when we exhibit a religious spirit and then communicate it with others, we're essentially injecting and spewing snake venom into them, potentially causing them harm, illness, or injury.

MY RELIGIOUS SPIRIT

I remember the fear of God coming over me when I first considered the possibility that I might have a religious spirit. Because I identify strongly with charismatic Christianity, I didn't think I had that kind of issue. But as I prayed and fiercely asked God for forgiveness regarding any religious-spirited attitudes in me, I had a shocking vision that led to a healing encounter.

In this vision I saw myself carrying a briefcase filled with my teachings and materials. I was immensely proud of it, thinking it was cutting-edge and fresh. I set it on a table and eagerly opened it to showcase my work to others. However, a snake suddenly leaped out of the briefcase and sprang at my face. I vividly remember grabbing the snake and throwing it away before it could sink its fangs into me.

This vision startled me so much it jolted me out of the encounter. Immediately I began to pray fervently, saying, "Oh, God, I'm so sorry. I didn't mean to think that my work was so superior. I repent of religious pride! Lord, forgive me, and wash me clean!" My prayer was filled with fiery intensity, even though it was the middle of the night. Then, as I prayed, something remarkable happened: my left ear, which had suffered hearing loss for most of my life, suddenly popped open! It was a remarkable experience. When I asked the Lord what had taken place, He loudly said, "Psalm 58:4: 'They have venom like the venom of a serpent, like the deaf adder that stops its ear'" (ESV).

That's when I realized that I had my own form of religiosity, thinking I was much more spiritually enlightened than those I considered "uptight Pharisees." My religious mindset had allowed a serpent to enter my life and literally stop up my hearing. However, as I repented and was delivered from it, my ear instantly popped open, and I could hear just as clearly in that ear as in the other.

It's worth noting that the Pharisees couldn't hear a word Jesus was saying even though He was the Messiah they had been looking for their whole lives! It seems the deaf adder had stopped up their ears too because of their religious spirit.

Just an added note: In the New Living Translation, Psalm 58:4 says, "They *spit venom like deadly snakes*; they are like cobras that refuse to listen" (emphasis added). Even the Bible says that people can spit snake venom! According to that translation, they also will refuse to listen, no matter what truth is being spoken to them.

SCALES ON YOUR EYES

When you have a prideful religious spirit, serpents not only can plug up your ears in the natural and block your ability to hear in the spirit but also blind your eyes with their scales.

Before he became an apostle, Paul was full of zeal for God. However, he had a religious spirit, which led him to fiercely harass the followers of Jesus. Let's refer to Paul's own words to see the extent of his religious tyranny against the early church:

> I am a Jew, born in Tarsus of Cilicia, but brought up in this city. I studied under Gamaliel and was thoroughly trained in the law of our ancestors. I was just as zealous for God as any of you are today. I persecuted the followers

of this Way to their death, arresting both men and women
and throwing them into prison, as the high priest and all
the Council can themselves testify. I even obtained let-
ters from them to their associates in Damascus, and went
there to bring these people as prisoners to Jerusalem to
be punished.

—ACTS 22:3–5, NIV

As you can see, Paul was deeply entrenched in religious-spirit-
edness, and he readily admitted it. In the Amplified Bible, Classic
Edition translation of this passage, he described himself as "ardent
[even a zealot]," saying, "[Yes] I harassed (troubled, molested, and
persecuted) this Way [of the Lord] to the death, putting in chains
and committing to prison both men and women" (vv. 3–4).

Paul thought he was serving God by killing and imprisoning
Christians. Yet unbeknownst to him, he was actually being controlled by demonic serpents, and they had put their scales on his
eyes so he couldn't see the truth.

Do you remember what happened to Paul on the road to
Damascus? Jesus appeared to him in the form of dazzling light and
knocked him to the ground. Paul was blinded by the encounter,
then taken into the city, where he did not eat for many days.

Thankfully the Lord sent a disciple named Ananias to pray for
him, and something remarkable happened—Acts 9:18 states, "And
instantly something like scales fell from [Saul's] eyes, and he recov-
ered his sight. Then he arose and was baptized."

When I read that, I said to the Lord, "Are You trying to tell me
those were serpent scales?" That is when the Holy Spirit reminded
me of who had trained Paul: one of the top Pharisees of the day.

Look again at what Paul said in Acts 22:3: "I studied under
Gamaliel and was thoroughly trained in the law of our ancestors"
(NIV). Acts 5:34 describes Gamaliel as a "Pharisee in the council
(Sanhedrin)...a teacher of the law, highly esteemed by all the people."

Again, what did Jesus and John the Baptist call the Pharisees?
Oh, "you brood of vipers!" The scales that fell from Paul's eyes

were snake scales. They had blinded him to the truth of Jesus being the Messiah, and he didn't even know it.

I've found these serpent scales can also cause someone to miss the will of the Lord, as they blind the victim to God's true path and calling in life. Many times the scales are responsible for breaking up ministry or business partnerships as these serpents target and cover the eyes of one of the parties, causing division and disagreement about the direction of the vision.

MIRACLE TESTIMONY

I've also witnessed, firsthand, extraordinary eye miracles happen when snakes and their scales are removed from people. Here is an astounding example.

For years a gentleman had suffered from a condition called chalazion. Since his childhood it had caused hard, painful growths to form on his eyelids that required surgical removal. Every few years he would have to go to the eye doctor and remain awake as his eyelid was numbed and the doctor used a scalpel to cut, drain, and remove the growths. These surgeries left him with scars all around his eyes.

When I interviewed this man at a tent event I was conducting in Moravian Falls, North Carolina, he reported that an incredible miracle had happened. While driving one day, he was listening to my teaching "Serpent and the Soul." A hard growth had started to form on his eyelid again, and it was very painful. As I shouted "Fire, fire, fire!" he suddenly witnessed in the spirit a snakelike entity slithering around inside his eye. (Since this man seemed to have no religious-minded attitudes, I think the religious spirit may have been in his bloodline.) As I continued to yell "Fire!" in the background, instructing people to take up serpents, the snake came out of his eye—then turned around to look at him!

Shocked, he came to a fast stop at the next intersection and grabbed the serpent by the head, pulling it out of his eye. He reported that the serpent was so long he had to use his other hand to get it out completely. (That is because the serpent had been there since his childhood.) The hard growth that had been forming on his eyelid and the pain that went with it disappeared as soon as the snake was removed.

As he testified that day, the entire audience broke into laughter when he added, "I threw it down and started shouting, 'Fire! Go into the abyss, and never return!' Then I looked around and saw people in other cars staring at me, and I was like 'Sorry, just removing a snake from my eye!'"

SIGNS YOU MAY HAVE A RELIGIOUS SPIRIT

Here are some common symptoms of those who have a religious spirit, adapted from a list by Mark DeJesus of Turning Hearts Ministries International.[1] Ask yourself these questions to see if you might have one yourself.

- Do you believe your revelations of Scripture are superior to everyone else's? This was something I struggled with.

- Are you emotionally rigid and inflexible? Such emotional stiffness can be a sign of a religious spirit.

- Do you find yourself frequently engaging in arguments, prioritizing being right over nurturing a loving relationship?

- Do you use theology as a means to avoid addressing your own brokenness? Some individuals use doctrinal arguments to deflect from their own woundedness, constantly telling others why they are wrong and pointing out Scripture passages to support their arguments.

- Do you pass judgments easily on people based on their outward appearances? Perhaps you judge individuals who might not meet your expectations in terms of dress, behavior, or background. It's important to remember that these are often the people who need your support the most.

I distinctly recall a time when I was newly released from prison and didn't have a wide selection of clothing. I had only a few outfits to wear. Excited to attend a church service, I walked up to the front desk designated for new visitors, extended my hand, and enthusiastically said, "I'm so thrilled to be here. I just got out of prison." Upon hearing those words, the woman behind the desk promptly withdrew her hand from mine, recoiled in shock, and said, "Are you sure you should be here?"

- Do you engage in religious activities, such as attending church regularly, without experiencing a heartfelt connection? Is your primary goal just to go through the motions, sing a few hymns, listen to a twenty-minute sermon, and say "Amen"? Also, are you indifferent to whether the people attending these activities actually experience healing and deliverance?

- Are you satisfied with religious programs that are more about routine activities than life-transforming experiences, lacking depth and genuine substance? If so, this might indicate a religious spirit.

- Do you find yourself frequently condemning and passing judgment on others, focusing solely on their flaws and not recognizing the gold within them, obscured by the dirt of their imperfections?

- Are you resistant to change, averse to anything new, thereby stifling the flow of the Holy Spirit? Is your preference for a certain worship style limiting your

openness to the diverse ways in which the Holy
Spirit may move? This can be a sign of a religious
spirit, with a potential python-like constriction on
your spiritual life.

- Do you exhibit stubbornness and pride, traits that
require personal repentance? Pride is a huge snake
magnet. I won't cover this extensively now, but in
later chapters I will directly connect it to a serpent
called Leviathan. However, just know that most
religious people are very prideful, which attracts
snakes.

- Are you inclined to impose a perfectionist form of
religion on others, viewing things as either 100 percent right or 100 percent wrong, without room for
a balanced perspective?

These are just a few indicators of a religious spirit.

ACTIVATION

If any of these resonate with you, or if you sense the Lord ministering to you regarding a religious spirit, let's activate change
right now. First go back over the previous list, and humble yourself
through sincere repentance. Then ask the Holy Spirit to show you
any other behaviors that would allow a brood of vipers to have
something in common with you.

Now pray this with me:

> *Lord Jesus, I refuse to be a person controlled by a brood of
> viper religious spirits. Cleanse me of every thought, motive,
> behavior, and response that bears the mark of religiosity.
> Rid me of any need to display religious manipulation or
> control, whether it's directed toward myself or others. In
> the name of Jesus, remove this serpent's influence from my
> life so that I may walk in freedom.*

Father, I also acknowledge any attitude in my life that has blinded me and allowed serpents to be released against me. I recognize that serpent scales have been placed on my eyes, leading to issues like cataracts, blindness, floaters, dry eyes, and glaucoma. Lord, I also come against the deaf adder that stops the ear, blocks me from hearing Your voice, and causes deafness, hearing loss, ear infections, ringing, and buzzing. Father, judge the evil in my soul that is allowing them to harm me, then judge those demonic snakes, in Jesus' name.

I also repent for any instances when I've harassed and mistreated fellow believers, akin to the actions of Paul when he persecuted and imprisoned Christians. I renounce the use of my words to throw stones to harm others, and instead I pull back those stones to prevent injury by blessing them. I beseech Your forgiveness, seeking Your grace and mercy, knowing it is by Your precious blood that I am cleansed. May my sins be washed away in the court of heaven. In Jesus' name, amen.

SNAKES AND MONEY

In Acts 16 we find the story about the apostle Paul encountering a woman with a spirit of divination:

> And it came to pass, as we went to prayer, a certain damsel possessed with a spirit of divination met us, which brought her masters much gain by soothsaying.
>
> —ACTS 16:16, KJV

This woman possessed the ability to foretell the future, which brought substantial financial gain to her masters.

First let's take a closer look at the term *divination* in the Greek; you might be surprised to find that it is the word *pythōn*.[2] Yes, a python spirit was controlling that woman; thus, the python spirit was also in charge of generating her masters' illegal financial gains.

So, if the python spirit has the power to bring illegitimate revenue to wicked individuals, what do you think it does to Christians? How does it affect *our* finances? Well, a python, in both the natural and spiritual worlds, wraps itself around its prey and slowly constricts, squeezing the life out until its victim is utterly vanquished. This is precisely what the python spirit does to your finances. It squeezes the life out of your business, ministry, church, online marketplace, social media platforms, and entrepreneurial endeavors. Unless you are delivered of this spirit, it will choke the life out of your finances until you're broke as a joke.

Some of the transgressions that could allow this spirit to operate in your life are poor stewardship, dishonest financial dealings, failure to tithe, a withholding spirit, a poverty spirit, idolatry (such as excessive shopping and spending), cheating, theft, extortion, or past involvement in gambling. Even if you've repented for gambling, if you haven't been fully healed of the addiction, that python spirit may still be active in your life.

We'll delve deeper into the python spirit in future chapters. However, it's essential to recognize that sins related to money are one of the factors that break open the protective hedge God has set around you. You can begin by seeking guidance from the Holy Spirit. Perhaps you're not tithing when you should be. Everyone's circumstances are unique, but remember, a serpent can infiltrate your finances and squeeze out your blessings when sins with money are involved.

THE SERPENT IN THE GARDEN AND FOOD

Another challenging topic is the sin we commit related to food. Yes, I know this can be tough to hear, but sinning with food can also create an opening in your hedge, allowing a serpent to slither in and bite you. Where do we find this in the Bible? Genesis 3 takes us back to the Garden of Eden, where the very first manifestation of a serpent in the Bible appeared.

Back in that garden so long ago, the snake "beguiled (cheated, outwitted, and deceived)" Eve into eating from the forbidden tree (Gen. 3:13). She saw the fruit, and it looked utterly delicious, so she took the bait. The serpent assured her, "You won't die if you eat it." But we know how that turned out, don't we? Both Adam and Eve died spiritually, and they both eventually aged, experiencing physical death when they were originally intended to be immortal.

Do you see the profound connection between food and the serpent? Right from the beginning, the serpent managed to cause the fall of all humanity using food as its weapon against us. Don't think for a moment that these serpents won't continue to exploit our vulnerability to food. Thus this facet of the serpents' strategy is clear: They will tempt you with food to drive you to overeat, to make you consume the wrong things—junk food, sugars, and all that unhealthy stuff. Why? So they can shame you with weight gain and hurt you physically, inflicting conditions like high blood pressure, diabetes, and obesity.

The serpents are using food, my friend, to gain entry. When you give in to their temptations by overeating and indulging in unhealthy choices, you are essentially inviting the serpents to come in and squeeze the life out of your health. You're allowing them to disrupt your ability to maintain a healthy weight and avoid the diseases associated with overeating.

ALCOHOL AND DRUGS

Another sin that connects people to serpents is the consumption of alcohol and drugs. Proverbs provides insight into this:

> Do not look at wine when it is red, when it sparkles in the wineglass, when it goes down smoothly. At the last it bites like a serpent and stings like an adder.
> —PROVERBS 23:31–32

Can you grasp the significance of the connection here? When you partake of alcohol and drugs, you're essentially creating a breach in God's protective hedge, allowing a serpent to enter and bite you.

Now, I understand that Paul advised Timothy to have a little wine for his stomach. However, there's a big difference between medicinal use and excessive recreational consumption of wine. Some might say, "I only have one glass of wine at night." But let's be honest: How large is that "one glass"? Does it gradually increase in size over time? Has it morphed into two or three? Are you even slightly affected by that one glass of wine? Or do you lose the ability to speak clearly, to drive safely? It's crucial to examine these aspects of your drinking habits.

Personally I've chosen to abstain entirely because I'm fully aware of the serpents' potential to exploit any opening to attack and control me. I suggest you pray deeply concerning this subject and get God's guidance on it for yourself.

ACTIVATION

Let's engage in a brief activation exercise. Consider whether you've been living under the influence of a serpent when it comes to food, alcohol, or drugs. Has it been whispering to you, tempting you to indulge in harmful things with promises like "Eat this. You won't die; you'll be just fine"?

Perhaps the voice you hear is pushing you to eat even when you're not hungry or to have a little alcohol when you go out to dinner. These spiritual entities can speak, as evidenced by the serpent in the garden who conversed with Eve and the woman possessed by the spirit of divination who spoke to Paul through the python that controlled her. Serpents talk, they tempt, and they aim to harm you—not just physically but also morally and socially.

Perhaps you have fought these addictions in the past but you have a good handle on them now. Unfortunately these snakes will stick around until they are cast out, as evidenced by Paul casting the python out of the woman with a spirit of divination. They want to stay for as long as they can to see whether they will have another opportunity to take over your life. Let's join in a prayer of agreement to fight them together. Repeat after me:

> *Lord God, I sense that I'm falling into the same deception that ensnared Eve in the garden. The serpent is tempting me with food, using it to condemn me, drive me to overeat, lead me to become unhealthy and overweight, and ultimately make me sick. I need the power of the Holy Spirit and Your authority to break free from this control. I break my agreement with the serpent that has tempted me to overeat and consume things I shouldn't. I declare that the serpent is judged and that I am breaking free from this negative eating pattern and moving toward my perfect weight, in the name of Jesus.*
>
> *Lord God, I also repent for allowing alcohol and drugs to become an access point through which the serpent can enter and hurt me. I recognize these addictions have broken through my hedge of protection, allowing the serpent to come in. Lord God, I declare that I am delivered through the judgment of the holy court, and I ask for healing in my physical body, removal of the addiction in my soul, and the elimination of the need for alcohol and drugs as a source of comfort. In Jesus' name, amen.*

WITCHES AND SNAKES

We now need to consider something vital: witches and their association with serpents. Grab your notepad because you're about to learn something transformative that you might not have known before.

Witches work with serpents. Remember the woman we mentioned earlier in Acts 16? Again, the word *divination* is the word *pythōn* in the Greek,[3] which means she was being controlled by a demonic snake. What exactly is divination? It's a form of witchcraft in which a person can foretell the future. So, this is an example that proves witches and snakes work together.

Now take a look at Leviticus 20:27, which states, "If there be a man or a woman in whom is a spirit of Python or of divination, they shall certainly be put to death: they shall stone them with stones; their blood is upon them" (DARBY). Here the Bible explicitly connects the python spirit with the spirit of divination.

Witches and serpents are collaborators in their dark works. Why is this knowledge essential? Because when you're battling serpents, you must also confront the witches and the witchcraft curses they've released against you. Here's how it works: witches cast curses, and serpents act as the enforcers, carrying out those curses. Let me illustrate this for you.

Job 3:8 says, "Let those curse it who curse the day, who are skilled in rousing up Leviathan." Witches, witch doctors, warlocks, sorcerers, and wizards are those who curse, and according to this verse, they are "skilled" in rousing Leviathan, whom the Bible calls the "twisting and winding serpent" (Isaiah 27:1). This shows that when a witch releases a curse against you, he or she is also awakening and inciting a serpent to carry out that curse!

Serpents are enforcers, the muscle behind curses. I can relate to this concept, as on the streets I was the "muscle" when it came to collecting debts on behalf of other drug dealers. When someone failed to pay a drug debt, the dealer instructed me to go and threaten the person, then collect the money that was owed. Many times I would forcefully take all the person's possessions to make sure the full payment was collected.

That's how serpents work. Witches cast a curse on you, then the snakes execute that curse—slowly and excruciatingly—until eventually everything is taken from you. Understanding this process is crucial because when you confront serpents, you are holding accountable not only the serpents who have tormented you but also the witches who cursed you.

Let me share a peculiar story that recently occurred, illustrating how witches engage in cursing while serpents enforce those curses.

A friend of mine recently told me about an herbal remedy from another country, claiming it could help with healing and maintaining good health, especially against illnesses like COVID-19 or the flu. This remedy was based on powerful local, natural herbs, and my friend explained that the secret recipe had been passed down to a Christian man. People who had used the antidote reported fast relief from flu-like and respiratory symptoms, including my friend himself.

Filled with excitement about this remedy, I went online and ordered a can, hoping it could help boost my immune system, as well as those of my ministry team, and fight off infection when we embarked on our tour.

As I read the instructions and prepared the mixture by adding scoops to water and stirring it, something quite unsettling happened. Upon adding the very first measure, I distinctly sensed a malevolent serpentine presence emerging from the powder. Immediately it raced up my arm and entered my breast.

Now, you might be wondering what on earth had just transpired. Well, I assure you, it was not my imagination. I physically felt it, and in the spiritual realm I could clearly perceive this serpent. (In later chapters I'll delve into how Leviathan is known to curse the breast and the womb.)

Thankfully I knew how to address this situation through spiritual discernment and intervention. Otherwise, had I not sensed it, seen it, or known what to do, there's a strong likelihood that, over time, I might have developed breast cancer as a result of this curse. I made specific decrees and cast that serpent out. I saw and felt it leave.

So, how does this relate to witches, curses, and serpents? There was nothing wrong with this mixture. However, in many parts of the country where this originated, witches engage in practices in which they curse the soil that farmers use to cultivate their crops.

Consequently, when farmers sow their seeds and grow their crops, people who consume those crops are affected by that curse.

Now, remember, it's the serpents who carry out the curses. The serpent was present in the mixture to enforce the curse against me. That's why, upon contact, I felt it ascend my arm and directly enter my breast, thereby cursing both my breast and womb (Job 3).

I share this story with you not to cause fear but to empower you with knowledge: when the enemy uses something like food or natural herbs, which God created for your good, to curse you, you have total authority over that assignment! Throughout this book I will share further shocking miracles that came about after breaking the assignments of witches and serpents consorting together to create sickness and disease.

WITCHES, SERPENTS, AND IDOLS

Another practice that allows holes to be broken in your hedge of protection is idolatry, which is directly connected to witchcraft, curses, and serpentine activity.

First Samuel 15:23 states, "For rebellion is as the sin of witchcraft, and stubbornness is as idolatry and teraphim (household good luck images)." In this verse rebellion is likened to witchcraft, and stubbornness is compared to idolatry. Witchcraft and idolatry are intricately connected!

Where do you think Jezebel derived her power and authority? It certainly didn't originate within her. Instead, her power was drawn from the idols she worshipped and the demon gods associated with them—namely, Asherah and Baal. Jezebel was a devoted idol worshipper, and behind every idol lies a demon spirit.

Now, why is this connection so significant? Well, many people fervently battle against Jezebel but get their butts kicked because, all the while, they have idols in their lives. If you have made anything into an idol, then you will have something in common with the demon gods behind those idols, which opens you up to being cursed by witchcraft.

Let's take this connection a step further.

> "Cursed is the man who makes an idol or a molten image, an abomination to the Lord, the work of the hands of the craftsman, and sets it up in secret." And all the people shall answer and say, "Amen."
>
> —DEUTERONOMY 27:15, NASB

Here's the crux of it: you're engaged in battle against Jezebel and witchcraft, yet you've overlooked repenting and getting cleansed from the idols that have taken up residence in your life.

Don't forget that the Bible says, "Like a flitting sparrow, like a flying swallow, so a curse without cause shall not alight" (Proverbs 26:2, NKJV). A witchcraft curse cannot alight unless it has a cause. If you want to prevent witchcraft curses from affecting your life and stop serpents from carrying them out, you must eliminate every cause, including any idolatry.

IDENTIFYING YOUR IDOLS

What idols are concealed in your life? Maybe there are expenditures or habits you haven't disclosed to anyone, including your spouse. Think about the times you've squirreled away some money to indulge in your own desires. Or perhaps it's excessive shopping— whether in person or online. Or maybe you spend endless hours scrolling through social media instead of consuming God's Word.

Take a moment to reflect on the idols in your life. Are they related to money, food, another person, or even yourself? Have you unwittingly turned your ministry into an idol, focusing on popularity and gaining "likes" rather than bringing the kingdom of heaven to earth?

I'm still a work in progress, and I continue to grapple with my own idols. However, I'm quick to repent when I recognize excess or imbalance in my life. I do this because I understand that idols provide the legal right for witchcraft curses to manifest and for serpents to enforce them.

Now identify your idols. Worship and pray in your spiritual language, allowing the Holy Spirit to reveal them to you, and then lay them before the Lord as we pray. Speak these words out loud:

Lord Jesus, I see it clearly now. I've been striving to combat witchcraft in my life while harboring idols that I've fashioned with my own hands. Your commandment is clear: "Have no other idols before Me. Make for yourself no graven images." Lord, purify my heart and soul from these idols I've been using to seek comfort. Forgive me of my sin, and judge every demonic altar of idolatry in my life. Let the curses lose their power, and forbid the serpents from carrying them out. I decree that I'm covered with Your blood and I am under Your free and unmerited grace. I place all my idols before You, Lord, and I receive the cleansing power of Your Holy Spirit and Your redeeming blood to eradicate idolatry from my life.

I also decree that I am under the power of the free and unmerited grace of God. Because the Bible says it's impossible to keep the whole Law, I need Your redemptive grace for my idolatry. I decree that where my sin of idolatry has increased and abounded, Your grace has increased the more to overshadow my sin and even superabound over it. I also decree Romans 3:20 and 24 over myself: It is written: "For no person will be justified (made righteous, acquitted, and judged acceptable) in His sight by observing the works prescribed by the Law....[All] are justified and made upright and in right standing with God, freely and gratuitously by His grace (His unmerited favor and mercy), through the redemption which is [provided] in Christ Jesus."

Heavenly Father, righteous Judge, I decree that because of the blood of Jesus and the power of His grace, I am acquitted of all charges of idolatry. In Jesus' name, amen.

Now boldly declare this:

I decree that Jesus has already borne the curse for me, rendering every witchcraft curse illegal! This is my testimony before this court. Therefore, I break these curses through the sacrifice of Jesus, and I ask this court to judge the demonic serpents that execute these curses in the name of Jesus. Now I, by decree, pull them off every area of my life. In Jesus' name, amen.

If you'd like to delve deeper into the topic of idolatry, consider exploring my book with Dr. Francis Myles called *Idols Riot!* It's a powerful resource that can help you break free from idolatry's grip. You can find it on katiesouza.com.

CHAPTER 3

SNAKES HATE FIRE

*Now Paul had gathered a bundle of sticks, and he
was laying them on the fire when a viper crawled out
because of the heat and fastened itself on his hand.*
—ACTS 28:3

THE FIERY PRESENCE of God has the incredible ability to force
serpents out of hiding. When we invite the presence of the
Holy Spirit—and His fire—into our lives, the snakes are
flushed out in the open, where we can effectively deal with them.

Genesis 3:1 says, "Now the serpent was more subtle and crafty
than any living creature of the field." Snakes are sneaky. They
know how to hide, so their presence in our lives is extremely difficult to detect. That's because serpents are masters of camouflage
technology.

Just think about snakes in the natural. Arizona boasts vast
desert regions, and within those deserts you'll find plenty of rattle-
snakes. Now, if you were to venture into that terrain, you would
have to be on the alert for a rattler, because spotting one in the

midst of sand, rocks, and dirt can be incredibly challenging. Their scales perfectly blend in with their surroundings. They are truly camouflage masters.

Now shift your focus to the Amazon rainforest, where massive anacondas, measuring more than twenty feet long and weighing up to five hundred pounds, reside.[1] Despite their great size these reptiles are difficult to detect because they move silently and their scales blend seamlessly with the jungle foliage. In fact an anaconda slithers with such stealth that its prey often remains oblivious to its presence until it is too late. By then the snake has already dropped down from above, encircled its unsuspecting victim, and tightened its grip until death is inevitable. These snakes are, without a doubt, masters of camouflage technology.

Let's apply these truths to demonic serpents. Once these snakes find an opening in your life, they will sneak up on you, blend in with your surroundings, then coil themselves around you—and you will be none the wiser until it's too late. It's only once they begin to tighten their coils and inject their venomous schemes into you, wreaking all sorts of havoc—troubles with your finances, a drain on your prosperity, turmoil in your marriage, sickness in your body, and much more—that you realize something is wrong. However, even then few of us grasp what's really going on. You're under a snake attack.

That's where the fire of God comes into play. It has the incredible ability to force these serpents out of their hiding places, where you can see them.

Millions of people throughout the world are walking around carrying demonic snakes and don't even know it! Let me prove it to you through this incredible story in Acts 28. In this passage we find the apostle Paul, who has just survived a shipwreck and been forced to swim to a beach during a horrific storm. Once ashore, he sets about gathering sticks to add to a fire the native islanders had built for warmth from the cold rain. However, in the process he unknowingly picks up a snake concealed within the bundle of sticks he has collected.

> After we were safe on the island, we knew and recognized that it was called Malta. And the natives showed us unusual and remarkable kindness, for they kindled a fire and welcomed and received us all, since it had begun to rain and was cold. Now Paul had gathered a bundle of sticks, and he was laying them on the fire when a viper crawled out because of the heat and fastened itself on his hand. When the natives saw the little animal hanging from his hand, they said to one another, Doubtless this man is a murderer, for though he has been saved from the sea, Justice [the goddess of avenging] has not permitted that he should live. Then [Paul simply] shook off the small creature into the fire and suffered no evil effects.
>
> —Acts 28:1–5

Let me unpack this for you. First of all, Paul was walking around carrying a deadly viper, and he didn't know it! How could that be? Because snakes are masters of camouflage technology! That snake was hidden in the sticks Paul had picked up.

It is very interesting that the word *bundle* (Greek *plēthos*) can mean "the multitude of people."[2] This tells me that a multitude of people are walking around carrying demonic serpents and don't realize it. Let me say it again: People all over the world—men, women, children; people of all walks of life—are unknowingly carrying demonic snakes around with them, and as a result they suffer from various afflictions such as breast cancer, diabetes, respiratory issues, back and neck problems, and unexplained bodily pains. Their marriages are breaking apart. Their businesses, churches, and ministries are shattered, yet they are unaware that demonic serpents are strategically wrapped around them, causing these afflictions.

Snakes are elusive, but the fire of God has the power to drive them out of hiding. When Paul threw the bundle on the fire, the heat drove that serpent out of its hiding place. It bit him, but he just shook it off and was miraculously left unharmed! This story underscores why the fire of God is of paramount importance in our battle against these serpents.

Snakes hate fire! Along with the flames one dangerous aspect of a forest fire is that venomous snakes may desperately slither away from the fire into residential areas.[3] When we immerse ourselves in the fire of God, it will drive out the snakes that we have unknowingly picked up during life's trials. The fire will force them to come out of hiding, where we can see them and get rid of them once and for all.

PERSONAL TESTIMONY

I recall a personal experience in which I discovered a troubling indentation in my breast, roughly half an inch deep. Seriously concerned, I asked, "What is this, Lord?" At the time, I was on tour and had just finished preaching. Immediately the Lord instructed me to immerse myself in His fire to reveal the root of the issue. So, after returning to my host's house around midnight, I played Misty Edwards' song "All-Consuming Fire" all night long. I'd sing along to the song, drift off to sleep, then wake up and continue singing.

The following morning I had a vision of a bloody bandage wrapped around my chest and a poisonous viper standing upright on its tail, with its characteristic triangular jaw, striking at me.

I asked, "What does this mean, Lord?"

He responded, "That serpent is putting breast cancer on you."

That's when I realized I was just like Paul. I had been carrying around a poisonous viper without knowing it, but the fire of God had driven it out into the open where I could see it.

At that moment I was so livid at the enemy. I even said out loud, "Satan, this time you've touched the goods, and the hubby is not going to be happy!"

Fortunately the Lord interrupted my anger with the next instructions: "You saw the head of the serpent. Now take it up as Jesus instructed you to do." So, I prophetically put on a metal glove (in case it still tried to bite), and I pulled it off my breast, then threw it into the abyss, commanding it to burn and never return.

Just an added note: I've found over the years that you need to soak in fire until you see the serpent's head. Sometimes these snakes are buried so deep in us that it takes a minute to get them to unwind. Once you see the head, however, you can remove its "headship" over you!

When I was back at home, the Lord instructed me to take Communion frequently over the next three days, as this would force the venom out of my body and the life-giving bread would bring regeneration to the breast. I obeyed, but each night, I experienced significant pain. As I lay in bed, I clutched my chest, thinking, "Oh my goodness, it's still there. I haven't gotten rid of it. I've only made it mad." Nevertheless, on the third morning, when I woke up and went to shower, I discovered the indentation had completely filled in! The pain I had felt was not the presence of the serpent but rather the process of my flesh regenerating.

It is of huge necessity that we regularly soak in fire to drive these hidden beasts off and out of our lives. That can look like anything from engaging in fiery worship, praying in fiery tongues, declaring scriptures concerning the fire of God, singing along to a song about Holy Spirit fire, to even listening to my *The Serpent and the Soul Fire Soak*, an MP3 with healing and deliverance music accompanying powerful fire scriptures and snake-trampling decrees.[4] When we declare and decree the fire-infused Scriptures, as well as engage in worship, praise, and thanksgiving, the fire of His divine presence descends on us, effectively driving these serpents out of their hideaways.

I've noticed significant surges in cancer cases worldwide. A huge percentage of these are snake-induced. I've had numerous conversations with individuals who have battled this disease. Cancer, even if defeated, often tries to come back. Case in point: Around five years after that encounter I attended a meeting with Tony Kemp, where he was teaching about the fire of God. As I sat there, I began fervently crying out, "Fire, fire, fire!" and praying fiercely in tongues. You see, I had been feeling oppressed, and I realized a serpent had come back to try to take me out with cancer again. As I persisted in pressing into the fiery presence, I actually could feel the serpents swirling in my breasts until they came out! Who knows what those demons might have done if I hadn't pressed into the fire! And that wasn't the last time they tried. (Note: don't be surprised if you feel swirling in your breasts, chest, and private areas as you are delivered of serpents while you read this book.)

The Fire of God Heals Your Soul

The fiery presence of God is required not only to drive the serpent out of hiding but also to consume the chaff within our souls that we have in common with these serpents. God created us as three-part beings: body, soul, and spirit. When you're born again in Christ, your spirit man becomes a new creation (2 Cor. 5:17), fully perfected in Him as His Holy Spirit comes to dwell with your spirit.

However, your soul doesn't become instantly perfected upon your regeneration. It can get wounded from things like sin, trauma, and issues that run through your bloodline. (See my book *Healing the Wounded Soul* for a full biblical understanding of this.)

Once your soul is wounded, demonic powers, including serpents, can gain the legal right to attack you. Those wounds act as a landing strip for the enemy to come into your life. In John 14:30, Jesus declared, "The prince (evil genius, ruler) of the world is coming....[He has nothing in common with Me; there is nothing in Me that belongs to him, and he has no power over Me.]" Frequently, the common ground that gives the enemy power over you is a wound in your soul stemming from sin or trauma. The good news is that the fire of God can cleanse your soul of these wounds.

The fire of God serves a dual purpose: it not only expels the serpents from their hiding places but also incinerates the baggage you carry within you. It consumes the chaff and eradicates those elements that might provide the serpent with common ground in you.

Look at this amazing story that perfectly illustrates this:

> In those days there appeared John the Baptist, preaching in the Wilderness (Desert) of Judea and saying, Repent

(think differently; change your mind, regretting your sins and changing your conduct), for the kingdom of heaven is at hand.

—Matthew 3:1–2

Then, starting in verse 7, it takes a striking turn:

But when he saw many of the Pharisees and Sadducees coming for baptism, he said to them, You brood of vipers! Who warned you to flee and escape from the wrath and indignation [of God against disobedience] that is coming? Bring forth fruit that is consistent with repentance [let your lives prove your change of heart]....And already the ax is lying at the root of the trees; every tree therefore that does not bear good fruit is cut down and thrown into the fire. I indeed baptize you in (with) water because of repentance [that is, because of your changing your minds for the better, heartily amending your ways, with abhorrence of your past sins]. But He Who is coming after me is mightier than I, Whose sandals I am not worthy or fit to take off or carry; He will baptize you with the Holy Spirit and with fire. His winnowing fan (shovel, fork) is in His hand, and He will thoroughly clear out and clean His threshing floor and gather and store His wheat in His barn, but the chaff He will burn up with fire that cannot be put out.

—Matthew 3:7–8, 10–12

Here we see John the Baptist at the Jordan River, baptizing people. Along came the Pharisees, whom he called a "brood of vipers." We touched on this earlier—this phrase implies they were religious men controlled by demonic serpents.

Notice that as soon as he saw them, he pronounced judgment, insisting they must repent: "Bring forth fruit that is consistent with repentance [let your lives prove your change of heart]" (v. 8). Again, this is where the significance of the blood and the cross of Jesus comes into play. Repentance is essential; if you are letting sin have dominion over you, then you must turn to the cross, where Jesus, the Seed of the woman, crushed the head of the serpent.

John emphasized this point to the religious Pharisees, saying, "You *must* repent." Furthermore, he warned them of impending judgment if they failed to do so, stating that if they didn't produce good fruit and a true change of heart, their trees would be felled and "cast into the fire," which indicates that fire is a judgment against snakes.

Then John continued with a warning about what the coming snake killer, King Jesus, would do when He arrived: "He Who is coming after me is mightier than I, Whose sandals I am not worthy or fit to take off or carry; He will baptize you with the Holy Spirit and with fire" (v. 11).

John was informing those serpent-controlled men that Jesus would have the antivenom to their demonic possession: the Holy Spirit and fire. They must repent and receive Christ's baptism of fire to escape the wrath of God.

I love what John says next, because it shows the power of fire to cleanse the Pharisees of everything in their souls that they had in common with those serpents in the first place. "His winnowing fan (shovel, fork) is in His hand, and He will thoroughly clear out and clean His threshing floor and gather and store His wheat in His barn, but the chaff He will burn up with fire that cannot be put out" (v. 12).

This news was not just for the Pharisees but also for the bride of Christ today. In His goodness and power Jesus separates the chaff from the wheat in our lives and burns up the chaff with unquenchable fire. What does this mean? Within each of us reside both good and bad attitudes and behaviors. The wheat symbolizes sound decision-making, positive emotions, healthy thoughts, and rational reasoning. But alongside the wheat we also have chaff—wrong thinking, harmful and detrimental conduct, and all the other junk in our trunks that warrants disposal. Fortunately Jesus divides the two and sets unextinguishable fire to the chaff.

The Holy Spirit and fire are soul-healing antivenom. When

Jesus baptizes you with the Holy Spirit and fire, that fire penetrates your being and consumes everything you share in common with demonic spirits, including serpents. Again, let's not overlook the context here. John the Baptist was addressing none other than the "brood of viper" Pharisees. When he spoke these words, he was imparting a deliverance message to them, urging them to repent so everything in them allowing the serpents to control their lives would be burned. We need to do the same.

This fire, when it blazes within you, consumes everything in your soul that connects you to a serpent, removing its control over you and thwarting its attacks. The fire doesn't merely expose the cunning, subtle serpent; it also brings profound healing to your soul.

Let's back up what I'm saying with evidence:

> When the day of Pentecost had fully come, they were all assembled together in one place, when suddenly there came a sound from heaven like the rushing of a violent tempest blast, and it filled the whole house in which they were sitting. And there appeared to them tongues resembling fire, which were separated and distributed and which settled on each one of them. And they were all filled (*diffused throughout their souls*) with the Holy Spirit.
> —ACTS 2:1–4, EMPHASIS ADDED

When that supernatural fire descended in the Upper Room, it didn't simply rest on top of the disciples' heads and flicker like beautiful flames; rather, it went somewhere. The fire "diffused throughout their souls." The Holy Spirit caused that fire to penetrate and disperse deep inside their inner beings to burn up everything that would have stopped those early believers from succeeding in their mission. This is why Jesus had the disciples tarry in the Upper Room *first* before they did anything else. He needed to get them filled with the Holy Spirit and fire not only so they would be empowered but also so they could be cleaned up before they went out into the ancient world to preach the gospel.

Now, consider the events of that remarkable day in the Upper Room. The fire descends, diffusing into their souls, baptizing them with both the Holy Spirit and fire. As a result they undergo a thorough cleansing and begin to demonstrate the power of walking in healed souls. Take Peter, for instance. The man who had once betrayed Jesus, who hid out of fear of the Jewish authorities, and who temporarily forsook his ministry to return to fishing—this same individual immediately rises to preach to a crowd of at least three thousand, where he then quotes from Scripture and brings them into salvation.

What caused a man consumed by fear, who had even denied Christ, to become a bold preacher of salvation before a multitude? The answer is fire—the fire of God that diffused into his soul, incinerating all the chaff within him. It eradicated his fear, his betrayal, his doubt, his sin, and everything else that held him captive, transforming him into a powerful servant of God. Oh, how I cherish this truth.

Now let's turn to Malachi 3:2, which declares, "But who can endure the day of His coming? And who can stand when He appears? For He is like a refiner's fire and like fullers' soap." Did you catch that? The fire of God refines you. His work cleanses you just like soap.

When the fire of God ignites, it accomplishes two vital things: it drives your serpentine adversaries out of their concealment, and it consumes the chaff that gives these demonic serpents a legal foothold to assail you in various aspects of your life—your body, marriage, finances, business, children, household, and so on.

The Courts of Heaven and the Serpent, Witches, and Idols

The Bible unequivocally states that we are seated in "heavenly realms" with Christ (Eph. 2:6, NIV). Part of this elevated position includes the remarkable privilege of wielding judicial authority and power over our adversaries, including serpents, from the courts of heaven.

The courts of heaven are also an antivenom to the serpent's bite. Let's substantiate this claim with Jesus' words:

> Behold, I give you the authority to trample on serpents and scorpions, and over all the power of the enemy, and nothing shall by any means hurt you.
> —Luke 10:19, nkjv

Believe it or not, this verse gives us direct permission and authority from Jesus to take these venomous vipers to court! The word *authority* used here (Greek *exousia*) can mean "the power of judicial decision."[5] Yes, you read that right. The authority Jesus has conferred on you is fundamentally jurisdictional, and it gives you the power to make and release legal decisions against all the powers of the enemy, including serpents.

Again, this verse says you have been given judicial authority "over all the power of the enemy"! So, legally you can also take those malevolent witches who are cursing you to court, along with the idolatrous spirits that plague and control you. In fact as a citizen of heaven (Phil. 3:20) you can arraign any diabolical force before the divine tribunal and assert your power of judicial decisions against it.

We considered the word *hurt* when we looked at Luke 10:19 in chapter 1. Now let's explore another nuance of this term. In the original context of this scripture, *hurt* implies "to be a criminal, to have violated the laws in some way."[6] It signifies that these serpents and all demons are essentially criminals; they have transgressed God's divine laws. What's the protocol for dealing with criminals? You take them to court, where justice is then administered on your behalf so they can no longer harm you.

Here's the thing: these serpents are constantly going to court, asserting that you are the transgressor, charging you with offenses like speaking ill of others, harboring bitterness, cursing people,

engaging in gossip, texting maliciously, or exhibiting traits and pat-
terns of rebellion, witchcraft, stubbornness, and idolatry. However,
as you step into the courts of heaven, armed with your judicial
exousia authority and the covering blood of Jesus' sacrifice, you
can confidently present your case. The enemy's accusations will
crumble, and you will emerge vindicated, free from guilt.

Through Christ we are made immaculate. Jesus exchanged His
perfect righteousness for our unrighteousness, ushering us into
the righteousness of God through our union with Him. Thus, in
heaven's divine courtroom, you are not a defendant. Rather, you
are a child of God who is in right standing with God because of
the work of Christ on the cross (Rom. 5:1; Eph. 2:16), possessing
authority to render legal judgments that will bind these demonic
serpents and thwart their malicious intentions.

So, how do you go to the courts?

I always like to soak in fire songs and my fire soaker for a few
days before I take those serpents and witches to court. It drives
them all out in the open and burns up the chaff in my soul so there
is no legal claim in me that's in common with them.

Mainly, decreeing the Word and worshipping are the ways to
build your faith to believe you have the right to ascend and operate
in the court (Eph. 2:6). As you worship, thanking God or praying
in your spiritual language, you will "enter into His gates with
thanksgiving, and into *His courts with praise*" (Ps. 100:4, NKJV,
emphasis added). There are gates and doors in heaven (Gen. 28:17,
NKJV; Rev. 4:1). You can enter through them and then access the
courts with your praise and worship.

Decree that you have the legal right to ascend into the courts
because you are seated in heavenly realms with Christ by virtue of
you being in Him (Eph. 2:6) and that you are a citizen of heaven
(Phil. 3:20), which gives you immediate access to your homeland.

Once you are there, start your testimony by covering any sins
with the blood. Revelation 12:11 succinctly states how we win a
court case: "And they overcame him by the blood of the Lamb and
by the word of their testimony" (NKJV). Testify out loud about the

power of the blood to crush the serpent's head! Take Communion while you do it. Decree that the blood has already washed you of all sin and that you are the righteousness of God in Christ! (If there is any idolatry or other sin of which you need to repent, do so while you take Communion.) Declare, "Jesus has already crushed the head of the serpent at the cross, and He already became a curse for me, so the causeless curse can't alight on me, according to Proverbs 26:2. This means the witchcraft curses are illegal!" Decree that you are under grace for every place you broke the law by worshipping idols, because where sin abounds, grace superabounds over it (Rom. 5:20)! Decree that you are already a new creation in Christ (2 Cor. 5:17), then worship and praise until you feel the release!

Once you have cleared the record of accusations the enemy has brought against you, it will be time to confidently exercise the exousia authority Jesus has imparted to you. Officially file a case against every witchcraft and idolatrous spirit and the serpents that are carrying out any curses against you. Release your power of a judicial decision against them. Ask the court to enforce your court filing through the "blood that speaks a better word" (Heb. 12:24, ESV), the power of God who is the "Judge of all the earth" (Gen. 18:25), the armies of angels, the cloud of witnesses, and the fire of God that burns up the enemy.

Then break those curses by the power of Jesus' name, and cast that serpent out by court decree in Jesus' name!

THE COURT OF THE ANCIENT OF DAYS

When confronting Leviathan and Python, two prominent demonic serpent principalities, I prefer to bring them before the court of the Ancient of Days, described in Daniel:

> I kept looking until thrones were placed [for the assessors with the Judge], and the Ancient of Days [God, the eternal Father] took His seat, Whose garment was white as snow and the hair of His head like pure wool. His

throne was like the fiery flame; its wheels were burning
fire. A stream of fire came forth from before Him; a
thousand thousands ministered to Him and ten thousand
times ten thousand rose up and stood before Him; the
Judge was seated [the court was in session] and the books
were opened.

—DANIEL 7:9–10

This section of Scripture undeniably validates the existence of
heavenly courts. Observe these clear words: "The Judge was seated
[the court was in session] and the books were opened." It couldn't
be more straightforward.

When it mentions "the books," understand that this includes not
only the books containing accusations from the enemy but also the
books filled with all that Christ has won for you and your destiny
in Him! These are the books documenting how He fulfilled the law,
how He shed His precious blood so that every handwritten requirement against you could be firmly nailed to the cross, and how He
utterly defeated the enemy by crushing the head of the serpent.

FIRE IN THE COURT

Now notice the intense levels of blazing fire that emanate from this
court: "His throne was like the fiery flame; its wheels were burning
fire. A stream of fire came forth from before Him" (Dan. 7:9–10).

Imagine the scene: The Ancient of Days, God Himself, who is
described as a judge about seventy times in the Bible, settles onto
the judge's bench in the court of heaven. It is ablaze with fire! The
fiery wheels attached to it enable His judgments to move back and
forth through time and space, burning up every bit of chaff in your
life right at the places it came in! Then, like massive flamethrowers,
streams of fire come from before Him to release fiery judgments
against every enemy you're battling, to burn them up like toast.

Do you see that? I love going into this court in godly fear and
absolute awe over the majesty and might of God! I play fire songs

and enter into fiery worship, then let the fire of God burn away any chaff in me that the enemy is using to accuse me. Daniel 7 says that in this court the power and dominion of the beasts are taken away (v. 12), and they are burned with fire (v. 11) as the fiery judgments of God incinerate these serpents, witches, and idols. Take that, Satan!

ACTIVATION

We're going to initiate a case in the court of the Ancient of Days, and we'll witness God's intervention because of Christ's blood and the exousia authority Jesus has bestowed on us.

Begin by praying in fiery tongues while you worship to some fiery music.[7] Praise and worship until you feel the fire. When you're ready, say this:

> Lord Jesus, I am seated in heavenly realms with You. By virtue of being in union with You, I declare that as a citizen of heaven, I can adjudicate and release legal decrees against the enemy now through the courts of heaven.
>
> Now I step into the court, and I earnestly ask that the Ancient of Days take His rightful seat, that the court be fully in session, and that the books be laid open. I ask that the court officer would not only read aloud all the accusations against me from the witches, warlocks, sorcerers, idolatrous spirits, and serpents but also loudly proclaim from the books everything Christ did when He crushed their heads at the cross, thus nullifying every accusation.
>
> As I enter this court, I know I will triumph over the enemy by the blood of the Lamb and my testimony. I commence this case by decreeing that every accusation the enemy has lodged against me, every entry recorded in those books, is covered by the blood of the Lamb. Every soul wound, every altar, every idol, every curse is cleansed. I decree that I am washed clean by the blood. I am already forgiven through Christ. I have already been

*declared righteous in Him. Every handwritten require-
ment that has been brought against me has already been
nailed to His cross, and through it He made a public
spectacle of the enemy.*

*Lord, I command Daniel 7:10 to come to fruition. May
the wheels of fire on your judge's bench go back throughout
time and space to every place a traumatic incident or sin
came upon my life and burn up the wounds right at their
roots. Burn up bitterness, every evil word or thought, idolatry, witchcraft, every religious spirit, pride, and all things
that would allow the serpent in. Lord Jesus, baptize me
with the next level of the infilling of the Holy Spirit and
fire! Take Your winnowing fork and separate the chaff
from the wheat right now. Burn up the chaff within me
with unquenchable fire—meaning no demonic strategy,
no opinion, no fear, no doubt, no serpent, no assignment, nothing can extinguish Your holy fire. It cannot be
quenched. I decree that You are doing all this even now!*

*Let the streams of fire emanating from the judge's
bench, flowing from Your throne, burn up the chaff in
my soul and eradicate any legal ground in the name of
Jesus. I decree that this fire is becoming a refiner's fire and
a fuller's soap to wash me totally clean. I decree that the
fire of God is diffusing into my soul right now to burn up
everything in common with any demonic spirit. Infuse my
soul with blazing fire! Consume it, Lord. Burn everything
away so that the enemy has no legal claim! I receive the
power of fire, in Jesus' name!*

Now fiercely pray in tongues while worshipping to the fiery
music you chose, and praise Him as the fire goes to work. Cry
out for the fire! Put a demand on a new level of the baptism of
fire. And decree that the fire is driving every serpent out of its
hiding place!

Then speak these words:

> *I declare fire against every hidden serpent. The fire is driving you out of concealment! You are being exposed by the fire! I will receive visions and dreams to discern how you have been undermining my health, stealing my finances, and tearing apart my marriage, family, business, and ministry. I decree it in the name of Jesus.*
>
> *Lord Jesus, I now release the exousia authority You imparted to me in Luke 10. I have the right to release the power of judicial decisions against the enemy. I hereby judge the entire work of the enemy that has been active against me. And by the power of the court, I cast these entities out, in Jesus' name! I decree and issue a restraining order to compel the enemy to cease any further attack on me, in the name of Jesus.*
>
> *I release the fiery judgments from the court of heaven against the beast, the enemy, and every serpent. As the flames emanate from the judge's bench, its wheels of fire, and the streams of fire, the power of their dominion is being fried to a crisp.*

Then say this:

> *I break every witchcraft curse, as they are illegal. Jesus already became a curse for me. And I put forth a case for full recompense to get back seven times everything these demonic powers took from me and my family. In Jesus' name, amen.*

CHAPTER 4

THE ANTIVENOM
POWER OF JESUS

*So the LORD God said to the serpent: "Because you
have done this...I will put enmity between you and the
woman, and between your seed and her Seed; He shall
bruise your head, and you shall bruise His heel."*
—GENESIS 3:14–15, NKJV

NTIVENOM IS "AN antibody therapy that can disable the
toxins within a specific venom if injected quickly into a
patient after a bite."[1] In this chapter we're going to delve
into the most powerful antidote to a deadly serpent bite: the work
of Jesus Christ on the cross.

Let's start by examining the very first prophecy in the Bible concerning Jesus. It's the moment when the serpent had just deceived
Adam and Eve into eating of the tree of the knowledge of good and
evil, causing all humanity to fall. Here God clearly declared the serpent's destiny due to his audaciousness to cause God's children to sin.

So the Lord God said to the serpent: "Because you have
done this, you are cursed more than all cattle, and more
than every beast of the field; on your belly you shall go,
and you shall eat dust all the days of your life.
                                                —GENESIS 3:14, NKJV

First of all, it's crucial to recognize that it's the enemy who is
cursed, not us! He went from standing upright to crawling on
his belly and eating dust for the rest of his life. We must begin
to embrace and decree the truth that the enemy has already
been judged!

Note: That old serpent took this curse literally. Your body is
made of the dust of the earth. As you will see throughout this
book, the serpent literally eats our bones, cartilage, and organs,
which causes disease of all kinds. One of the many reasons we need
to learn these biblical precepts is so we can stop his assault.

The second part of God's declaration against the serpent went
like this:

And I will put enmity between you and the woman, and
between your seed and her Seed; He shall bruise your
head, and you shall bruise His heel.
                                                —GENESIS 3:15, NKJV

I love that the very first prophecy in the Bible is about Jesus
Christ, the Seed of the woman, crushing the head of the serpent.
That shows you the importance of what you're learning in this
book. If Jesus' first task was to trample the serpent, then it should
also be ours.

When did this crushing take place? It transpired at the cross!
The significance of the cross in totally defeating the enemy is highlighted in Colossians 2:15, which states, "[God] disarmed the principalities and powers that were ranged against us and made a bold
display and public example of them, in triumphing over them in
Him and in it [the cross]."

The Bible is clear that Jesus came to destroy the works of the enemy (1 John 3:8), and He fully accomplished His mission by being nailed to that implement of crucifixion. It was on the cross that Jesus took back everything the snake had slithered away with in the garden, making a public spectacle of him forever. Named in Scripture as "the last Adam" (1 Cor. 15:45), Jesus redeemed all the first Adam lost to the deception of the old serpent. On the lowly hill of Golgotha the Son of God, naked and bleeding, invaded time on a mission to crush that transgressor's skull.

Often I will soak to one of the crucifixion stories from my audio Bible to get rid of a snake attack. As I listen, I pray along with the account and use the power of that testimony to achieve a breakthrough. It's amazing how this simple exercise brings me the deliverance I need. That is because I'm tapping in to the moment when Jesus performed the crushing, freeing us forever. (Many audio Bible tracks are available on YouTube for free.)

You must use the power of the cross as a weapon against these serpents, decreeing that you are innocent of their charges because of it and that they must therefore unwind as you trample on them with the authority Jesus has imparted to you through His ultimate sacrifice.

THE ACCUSATIONS HAVE BEEN PERMANENTLY BLOTTED OUT

The snake's forked tongue is always hissing, "They are lawbreakers just like their parents, Adam and Eve." The law is his strength against us (1 Cor. 15:56). Without our infringing of it, he wouldn't have a case.

Yet the task of daily struggling to keep the law seems absolutely insurmountable. Good thing Jesus did it for us!

> For what the law could not do in that it was weak through the flesh, God did by sending His own Son in the likeness of sinful flesh, on account of sin: He condemned sin in the flesh, that the righteous requirement of the law

might be fulfilled in us who do not walk according to the
flesh but according to the Spirit.

—ROMANS 8:3–4, NKJV

God sent His one and only Son here to die. Why? Our flesh
was too weak to keep the whole law, so Christ had to come in the
likeness of human flesh to condemn sin. Imagine the King of glory
lowering Himself to the state of a frail human to redeem us. In that
submitted body Jesus did not sin, thus perfectly fulfilling the law
on our behalf—something Scripture says we could never do.

To prove this, the Book of James declares this sobering truth:

> For whosoever keeps the Law [as a] whole but stumbles
> and offends in one [single instance] has become guilty of
> [breaking] all of it.

—JAMES 2:10

No one can maintain the whole law. It's literally impossible.
The only Person in the history of the world who could accomplish
this monumental task was God in the flesh. As Jesus walked the
earth in a human body, He satisfied every jot and tittle of the law
flawlessly, qualifying Him to become the Lamb without spot or
blemish (1 Pet. 1:19), the atoning sacrifice for all people.

YOUR SINS HAVE BEEN COMPLETELY BLOTTED AWAY

The vastness of Christ's accomplishment on the cross must not
be understated. When we spend more time meditating on our sin
than contemplating the One who took it from us, we will be positioned to grovel at Satan's feet instead of to worship at the Savior's.
Let's remind ourselves of the completeness of His labor:

> You who were dead in trespasses and in the uncircumcision
> of your flesh (your sensuality, your sinful carnal nature),
> [God] brought to life together with [Christ], having

> [freely] forgiven us all our transgressions, having can-
> celled and blotted out and wiped away the handwriting of
> the note (bond)....This [note with its regulations, decrees,
> and demands] He set aside and cleared completely out of
> our way by nailing it to [His] cross.
>
> —COLOSSIANS 2:13–14

Christ has brought you from death to life by completely wiping out the note that was against you. And what is this "handwriting of the note"? It's the written law "with its legal decrees and demands which was in force and stood against us (hostile to us)" (v. 14). The law is hostile because you can't keep it, and this failure creates opposition against every part of your life. The word *hostile* can mean "of or belonging to a military enemy,"[2] conveying that your inability to carry out the law enables the enemy to implement military aggression against you.

Nevertheless, through Christ your transgressions have been freely forgiven, canceled, and blotted out! Jesus nailed the law to His cross by fulfilling it in Himself. In doing so, He set aside and cleared away the regulations, decrees, and demands that came with it. So, say bye-bye to the accusations from the serpent's tongue.

Please understand that the law is holy, just, and good (Rom. 7:12). The apostle Paul said, "If it had not been for the Law, I should not have recognized sin or have known its meaning" (v. 7). The law shows us what is sin and what isn't. It's our guide. Nonetheless, even Paul said, "The very legal ordinance which was designed and intended to bring life actually proved [to mean to me] death" (v. 10).

Though the law was perfect, it did not bring life, as Paul so aptly stated. Because of our miserable failure to keep it, a new covenant had to be provided in Jesus.

YOU ARE DEAD TO THE LAW THROUGH JESUS

The price Jesus paid on the cross was so all-encompassing that now you are no longer under the power of the law but belong to the One who fulfilled it on your behalf.

> Likewise, my brethren, you have undergone death as to the Law through the [crucified] body of Christ, so that now you may belong to Another, to Him Who was raised from the dead in order that we may bear fruit for God.
> —ROMANS 7:4

You are totally dead to the law now. It can't be held over your head anymore. When Christ's body was torn apart through the whipping and the piercing nails, those legal decrees and demands were simultaneously shredded to bits, and now the Bible boldly proclaims this:

> But now we are discharged from the Law and have terminated all intercourse with it, having died to what once restrained and held us captive. So now we serve not under [obedience to] the old code of written regulations, but [under obedience to the promptings] of the Spirit in newness [of life].
> —ROMANS 7:6

When I read that verse, I weep. In a legal sense the word *discharge* can mean "canceling an order of a court," as well as "releasing someone from the custody or restraint of the law."[3] You have been discharged from the jail cell the enemy kept you in through his accusations of your lawbreaking. The power of Christ's blood sacrifice was so formidable that it legally dissolved the covenant that bonded you to the law, releasing you from its power and consequences forever, but you must believe it and decree it. Since you have been discharged from the law, the serpent can never put his filthy scales on you again.

All binding connections you had with the law have been terminated; now you live under the obedience and control of the Holy Spirit—when you submit. The Spirit has written God's law on your heart, which leads you into righteousness more than the old code of regulations ever could. Now, through leaning into the control of the Holy Spirit, you can walk in the power of new life, possessing power over sin.

> Now, then, there is no condemnation to those who are in Christ Jesus; who do not walk after the flesh, but after the Spirit. For the Law of the Spirit of life, Who is in Christ Jesus, has freed me from the Law of sin and of death.
> —ROMANS 8:1–2, RGT

> You are not ruled by the power of sin. Instead, the Holy Spirit rules over you.
> —ROMANS 8:9, NIRV

As you read the previous verses, remind yourself that one of the fruits of the Spirit is self-control. When you choose to be governed by His fruit, refusing to walk after the flesh, then you are choosing to abide in this power over sin.

THERE IS NO SPOON

Ultimately we need to understand that because of Christ, we are no longer under the power of sin—period. Thus, you don't have to cave in to temptation (1 Cor. 10:13) and submit to sin. Look at this bold claim in Colossians 2:

> Through our union with him we have experienced circumcision of heart. All of the guilt and power of sin has been cut away and is now extinct because of what Christ, the Anointed One, has accomplished for us.
> —COLOSSIANS 2:11, TPT

Sin's dominance has been cut away, and now it is totally extinct through Christ! *Extinct* means destroyed, exterminated, no longer in existence. Believe it or not, sin's power over you doesn't exist. Jesus has completely stripped its power to dominate your life. Now you must choose to believe and act.

This outrageous truth reminds me of an iconic scene in the movie *The Matrix*, starring Keanu Reeves. He is with a young boy who, with no effort, is bending a metal spoon using only his mind. As the child tutors Keanu's character, Neo, to do the same, the youth speaks a mind-blowing reality: "Do not try and bend the spoon. That's impossible. Instead, only try to realize the truth.... There is no spoon."[4]

The law, like the spoon, is unbendable. It's impossible for us to break its power off our lives. Therefore, we must recognize the truth: because of Christ, there is no spoon.

The young boy closed by saying, "Then you'll see that it is not the spoon that bends; it is only yourself." Neo was called to disbelieve what his senses were telling him. There it was, the metal spoon, right in front of his face. He was looking at it with his own eyes, touching the cold metal with his hands. How could there be no spoon? Yet when he embraced that truth, he, too, was able to bend it with ease.

You are called to believe what seems impossible, no matter how you think or feel. All the guilt and power of sin has been cut away and is now extinct because of what Christ, the Anointed One, has accomplished for us. The legal ramifications of this are vast. It means the enemy no longer has the legal right to file a case against you and arrest your life in any way. Look at this fabulous confirmation in Colossians 2:

> He canceled out every legal violation we had on our
> record and the old arrest warrant that stood to indict us.
> He erased it all—our sins, our stained soul—he deleted it
> all and they cannot be retrieved!
>
> —COLOSSIANS 2:14, TPT

Your criminal record is totally clean! It has been deleted and cannot be retrieved! Do you understand the implications of this? No more demonic-inspired sickness, lack, disease, disorder, strife, or warfare. The more you dismantle your own false belief systems, the more you will manifest this truth.

You may still be thinking there is no way this is really possible. After all, what do you do when you "break weak" and sin? How do we reconcile that seeming reality with the truth that we are dead to sin and it has no power over us? This is why we desperately need grace.

THE POWER OF GRACE

Did you know that grace is the power that enables you to partake of all Jesus accomplished on the cross? It's a super-antivenom against the serpent. Ephesians 2:8–9 says, "For by grace you have been saved through faith, and that not of yourselves; it is the gift of God, not of works, lest anyone should boast" (NKJV).

When the Bible talks about salvation by grace through faith, it includes much more than being saved in Christ. The word translated as "saved" is the Greek word *sōzō*, which means "to save, i.e., deliver or protect…heal, preserve…(make) whole."[5] This indicates that your salvation includes healing for your body; the ability to be made whole, preserved, and healthy; and even deliverance and protection from the enemy.

Grace is the power that transmits these blessings and more into every part of your existence. This includes the truth that Jesus fulfilled the law on your behalf, caused the power of sin to be extinct, and crushed the serpent's head at Golgotha.

Because your salvation happened by grace through faith alone and not by your own works, as the previous passage states, you are not left alone to fight off sin in your own strength. No, grace is here to help you when you lean into it. Look at this beautiful verse of Scripture:

> Then Law came in, [only] to expand and increase the tres-
> pass [making it more apparent and exciting opposition].
> But where sin increased and abounded, grace (God's
> unmerited favor) has surpassed it and increased the more
> and superabounded.
>
> —ROMANS 5:20

When the law is transgressed, it excites "opposition" against you. Some of the meanings of that word are "hostile or contrary action or condition" and "a group of adversaries."[6] Lawbreaking excites and enables the adversary's actions against your life. But hallelujah, grace triumphs over the law! Just reading this brings such reassurance to the weary soul. When sin overpowers your resolve in the truth of Christ's victory, you can rest in knowing that God's unmerited (unearned) grace will surpass the consequences of the law. In fact it will even increase the more and superabound over it.

No accusation of lawbreaking can stand when you understand and apply the grace of God. When I forget or fail to walk in the truth of Jesus' making sin's power extinct, I immediately repent and rush to grace, meditating on it, believing it, and decreeing it over my sin—then quickly the serpent attack dissipates.

GRACE BREAKS THE POWER OF SIN

Because grace imparts to you the full work of the cross, it can break the dominion of sin off you too.

> For sin shall not [any longer] exert dominion over you,
> since now you are not under Law [as slaves], but under
> grace [as subjects of God's favor and mercy].
>
> —ROMANS 6:14

A slave is a person who is the legal property of another and is forced to obey his or her master. Before God's glorious grace came, you were essentially the legal property of the law. It had dominion over you. You were forced to follow and obey it, even though you could not. But grace freed you from that bondage. Instead, you are now a subject of God's favor and mercy.

Second Corinthians 5:21 says that Christ, who knew no sin, became sin for you so that you could be made the righteousness of God in Him. That's important, because God does not look at righteous people as lawbreakers. Grace is the power that imputes His righteousness to you and then makes sin's power extinct.

THE GRACE COURT

The Scripture states we are acquitted of criminal charges through the power of grace (Rom. 5). This is reason to point out one of the most powerful courts in heaven's judicial system: the Grace Court.

Again, in the world there are many different categories of courts—civil, criminal, family courts, and more. Everything on earth is fashioned after the governmental pattern of heaven. So, it's no surprise there are many different types of courts in the heavenly realms. According to Scripture one of the most effective is what I call the Grace Court.

The writer of Hebrews 4:16 declared, "Let us therefore come boldly to the throne of grace, that we may obtain mercy and find grace to help in time of need" (NKJV). The Greek word for *throne* in this verse is *thronos*. It is a "seat" used by kings or judges that is "equivalent to [a] tribunal or bench."[7] (See also Matthew 19:28; Luke 22:30; and Revelation 20:4.) The throne in Hebrews 4 is not just a chair on which God sits. Rather, it is the bench from which the judge of all the earth releases justice and mercy for His people through His glorious grace!

Have you ever heard the expression "throw yourself on the mercy of the court"? That's what happens in this courtroom. Here all decisions and rulings are based on the grace and mercy of God. Therefore, if you are struggling with lawbreaking, this is the place to find justice and reprieve. The Bible says that "mercy triumphs over judgment" (Jas. 2:13, NKJV), and grace always trumps the law. Hence, in this court, you can never lose!

Grace will actually enable you to be declared innocent of every charge that has been lodged against you in court.

> We are justified (acquitted, declared righteous, and given a right standing with God) through faith....Through Him also we have [our] access (entrance, introduction) by faith into this grace (state of God's favor) in which we [firmly and safely] stand.
>
> —ROMANS 5:1–2

Notice that by the power of grace you have been not only justified with God but also acquitted of every single charge the serpent would file against you. When the enemy accuses you of breaking the law, you can come right back at him and say, "Yes, but because of Christ and His grace, I am totally guiltless!"

GET TO KNOW GRACE

Did you know that Psalm 92 says the righteous will "flourish in the courts of our God. [Growing in grace] they shall...bring forth fruit" (vv. 13–14)? This indicates your need to cultivate massive amounts of knowledge concerning grace and the jurisdictional power available to you in Christ. This growth will lead you to thrive in your ability to win in court and experience the full manifestation of God's goodness in every area of your life.

This is one of the reasons Paul commends believers to become "progressively acquainted with and recognizing more strongly and clearly the grace of our Lord Jesus Christ (His kindness, His gracious generosity, His undeserved favor and spiritual blessing)" (2 Cor. 8:9).

You must grow in your awareness and knowledge of His endless grace. Failure to do so could be devastating, especially when you need a breakthrough in the courts over serpents. As you dive into grace, you will find that it's like the sea, boundless in its beauty and depths. There is no way to find the bottom of grace. Its sunken treasures are waiting to be discovered by those who would search them out.

The Cornerstone of the Grace Court Is Christ

The Grace Court adjudicates every legal decision based on the power of Christ's crucifixion, His shed blood, and grace super-abounding over the law. Thus, to ignore grace as a vital need in your everyday life is to severely slight the gift God gave us in Christ. Look at what Paul said about it:

> [Therefore, I do not treat God's gracious gift as something of minor importance and defeat its very purpose]; I do not set aside and invalidate and frustrate and nullify the grace (unmerited favor) of God. For if justification (righteousness, acquittal from guilt) comes through [observing the ritual of] the Law, then Christ (the Messiah) died groundlessly and to no purpose and in vain. [His death was then wholly superfluous.]
>
> —Galatians 2:21

The very purpose of grace is to trump the law. Therefore, you should never nullify its power by setting it aside or diminishing its importance. Paul says that if you do that, you will be "severed" from Christ (Gal. 5:4)! Why would he say something so drastic? Because if you believe you can be justified and kept in right standing with God through your own strength, you don't need Jesus or His sacrifice!

That would be a punch in the face to our Lord, who was whipped, beaten, and pierced through with nails up to nine inches long so you could be declared righteous in God's sight. In Galatians 5:4, Paul continues the same thought. Let's look at the entire verse: "If you seek to be justified and declared righteous and to be given a right standing with God through the Law, you are brought to nothing and so separated (severed) from Christ. You have fallen away from grace (from God's gracious favor and unmerited blessing)."

Separating from Christ's sacrifice will greatly diminish your ability to live in peace and wholeness. It will also negatively affect your ability to get a swift decision from the court, as carrying a greater revelation of grace will release more of its power into your case.

IDOLATRY IS LAWBREAKING 101

As we continue to look into the power of grace and the Grace Court, remember we are dealing with accusations that are also connected to idolatry and witchcraft. Let's touch on idolatry first.

Recall the first and second commandments of God: "You shall have no other gods before Me" (Exod. 20:3, NKJV). And "You shall not make for yourself any idol" (v. 4, AMP).

Idolatry is the violation of the first two laws God gave to Moses. When you partake of his evil agenda, Satan has legal standing to indict you in the courts. In fact idolatry is the number one accusation Satan levies against you in the courts of heaven, as it so severely breaks God's covenant laws.

As I have briefly touched on already, idolatry is also intricately intertwined with witchcraft and serpents. Just recall Deuteronomy 27:15: "Cursed is the man who makes an idol or a molten image, an abomination to the LORD, the work of the hands of the craftsman, and sets it up in secret" (NASB).

If you have any idols in your life, then a witchcraft spirit can curse you, and the serpent will carry it out. It's a three-cord demonic strand that most believers do not understand. Consequently they take on Jezebel and get a beatdown because their lives have something in common with her: idolatry.

WITCHCRAFT AND THE LAW

When it comes to witchcraft, you are in danger of having something in common with it and losing your case if you forego grace and fall into the trap of trying to keep the law through your own efforts. Paul makes this very clear in the Book of Galatians:

> O you poor and silly and thoughtless and unreflecting and senseless Galatians! Who has fascinated or bewitched or cast a spell over you, unto whom—right before your very eyes—Jesus Christ (the Messiah) was openly and graphically set forth and portrayed as crucified? Let me ask you this one question: Did you receive the [Holy] Spirit as the result of obeying the Law and doing its works, or was it by hearing [the message of the Gospel] and believing [it]? [Was it from observing a law of rituals or from a message of faith?] Are you so foolish and so senseless and so silly? Having begun [your new life spiritually] with the [Holy] Spirit, are you now reaching perfection [by dependence] on the flesh?...Then does He Who supplies you with His marvelous [Holy] Spirit and works powerfully and miraculously among you do so on [the grounds of your doing] what the Law demands, or because of your believing in and adhering to and trusting in and relying on the message that you heard?
>
> —GALATIANS 3:1–3, 5

Paul accused the Galatians of being "bewitched" and having a "spell" cast over them because they believed God would perform miracles on their behalf only if they were doing what the law demanded. They forgot that the Holy Spirit was poured out on them just through their faith in Christ, not by observing a law of rituals.

Do you see the connection between attempting to keep the law in your flesh and witchcraft? Paul didn't mince words, stating very clearly that trying to reach perfection through dependence on the flesh would invite a witchcraft spirit to cast a spell, bewitching and cursing you.

This is yet another reason to stay immersed in grace. It destroys the power of idolatry and witchcraft in your life.

GRACE VS. REPENTANCE

The one thing that used to bother me so much about the courts of heaven was the excessive repentance that seemed to be required to win a case. Don't get me wrong; I *love* repentance! And I whole-heartedly endorse this vital practice! I think the body of Christ and the world need to do more of it. Then we would not be encrusted in the filth in which we are currently walking.

In fact sometimes deep repentance is required to break the back of ingrained sin. The Bible says our conscious minds are cleansed of "dead works" and "lifeless observances" by His blood (Heb. 9:14). Dead works can be anything from sin to fruitless endeavors in your life, while lifeless observances represent the law and the works of your flesh to keep it. Many times it takes a deep blood soak with repentance to dig these things out at their roots.

However, I also think we get out of balance by staying stuck in repentance while failing to bring in the victorious good news of Christ's grace and our ability to be acquitted of sin through its power. Excessive, repetitive repentance with no grace or aware-ness of the ultimate power of Christ's sacrifice to destroy sin can become a work of the flesh, an attempt to seek to be justified by a ritual.

I've told this story before, but I believe it is worth repeating here. When I first started pursuing healing, I would spend endless hours repenting of my sins. Even if I didn't think I was sinning in that area, I would still repent. During those times I always felt as if it was never enough. I even repented for things I hadn't done, just in case.

One day while embroiled in this overwhelming process, I saw a vision. I was trapped in a laundry machine that was stuck on the wash cycle. I saw myself churning around and around, liter-ally drowning in the sudsy water. I snapped out of the vision in a panic and immediately heard the Lord say, "Enough repenting—now believe!"

We can turn repenting into a work of the flesh by not believing in Christ's finished work while we do it. This is an affront to His sacrifice and allows witchcraft to come in and curse us. Yet by not repenting, we can leave an opening in the hedge of protection; then the snake can come in to bite us.

To repent or not to repent—that is the question.

So which is it? Do we need to repent or just rely on grace? I firmly believe it is both! Look at how these amazing verses connect repentance with the release of God's grace that has been freely given to us:

> Blessed [forgiven, refreshed by God's grace] are those who mourn [over their sins and repent], for they will be comforted [when the burden of sin is lifted].
> —MATTHEW 5:4, AMP

> Blessed [forgiven, refreshed by God's grace] are you who weep now [over your sins and repent], for you will laugh [when the burden of sin is lifted].
> —LUKE 6:21, AMP

Notice these verses say God's grace refreshes you *when you repent.* I love jumping into my pool after getting sweaty and grungy from a long day of working outside. It's so refreshing and energizing to be submersed in that cool water. That's what repentance does: it removes the grunge of sin so grace can invigorate, rejuvenate, and restore you.

So, how much repentance is enough? Look again at the marvelous verses in Matthew 5 and Luke 6. They show that those who repent are refreshed by God's grace and are comforted "when the burden of sin is lifted." That's your clue! When you feel the burden lift, you've hit the sweet spot!

One of the most powerful verses in the Bible about repentance is found in the Book of James, which says that God "gives grace to the humble" (4:6, ESV). There is no better way to humble yourself than through repentance. It's no coincidence that in the verses preceding this, James challenges the reader to stop partaking in quarrels, jealousy, strife, envy, and adultery. Sounds like some peeps needed to repent. Those who advocate only for grace haven't had the revelation that repentance causes more grace to be released.

ENTERING THE GRACE COURT

Let's get ready to enter the Grace Court. Have Communion ready as you go in. Always begin with worship and praise, because the Bible instructs you to "enter into His gates with thanksgiving, and into His courts with praise" (Ps. 100:4, NKJV). So, begin by engaging with the Lord through worship—singing, dancing, praising, thanking Him, and praying in the Spirit.

Next you may want to kneel in worship before the Lord as you prepare to receive Communion and be cleansed of any sin connected to idolatry, witchcraft, and the serpents. Say this prayer:

> *Lord Jesus, as I bow before You in total humility, I ask the Holy Spirit to search my heart for any transgressions that connect to these demonic spirits that are assaulting me. My desire, Lord, is to walk in the righteousness You have already won for me. Create in me a clean heart, and renew a right spirit within me. I repent of any sins in my life or bloodline connected to idolatry, the rebellion and bitterness of witchcraft, and any sins I've committed that are connected to demonic snakes. Your body and blood are cleansing my soul of those sins so that they will never control me again.*

Take a moment to meditate on this. Press into His presence. Meditate on the cross and Christ bleeding out in your place so you can be set free. Now say this:

> *Lord, I decree as I eat this bread that represents Your flesh that I am doing it in remembrance of the moment You crushed the serpent's skull on the cross. I decree Romans 7:4 over myself: through the crucified body of Christ, I*

have undergone death to the law. Every accusation the enemy has filed of my lawbreaking is destroyed because of Christ's death on the cross. I partake of His crucified body—the Bread of Life—now, and I rejoice in its power to free me from the power of the law.

I also admit that my flesh was too weak to keep the law. Thus, God sent His Son in the likeness of sinful flesh, on account of sin, to condemn the sin in the flesh. Because Jesus came in a human body, the righteous requirement of the law was fulfilled for me (Rom. 8:3–4, NKJV). So, I decree that as I partake of the flesh of the Son, the living Bread, Jesus has fulfilled the law on my behalf and that therefore no charges of my lawbreaking can be held against me.

I also declare that the bread of Communion is forcing the serpents' venom out of every organ, cell, bone, and joint in my body and that Christ's body is bringing life to any place the enemy has put sickness or death on me, in Jesus' name.

Now partake of the bread. Then as you hold the cup of His blood in your hand, say this:

Lord, Your blood was poured out for my sins, causing the serpents' power in my life to be crushed. Partaking of this cup causes that crushing to take place now! I decree the words of Colossians 2 over myself: I was dead in trespasses and in the uncircumcision of my flesh, but God has brought me to life together with Christ, having freely forgiven me of all my transgressions. I decree that His blood has canceled, blotted out, and wiped away the handwriting of the law with its regulations, decrees, and demands that were against me. I declare that Jesus has totally set aside and cleared the law completely out of my way by nailing it to His cross and that through my partaking of His blood, this decree becomes effective.

> *I decree that through my union with Him, I have experienced a circumcision of the heart. "All of the guilt and power of sin has been cut away and is now extinct because of what Christ, the Anointed One, has accomplished" for me"* (Col. 2:11, TPT).
>
> *Now, Lord, I as I drink of Your cup, I declare Romans 7:6 over myself. I decree I am now discharged from the law and have terminated all bonds with it. By going down in death with Christ at the cross, I have now died to what once restrained and held me captive. The word* discharge *means "canceling an order of a court" and "releasing someone from the custody or restraint of the law."*[8] *I decree that the judge of all the earth is now canceling any case that has been filed against me by the enemy because of the blood of Jesus! I also declare that I have been released from the enemy's custody because I am no longer under the restraints of the law.*
>
> *Now I declare that I serve under obedience not to the old code of written regulations but to the promptings of the Spirit in newness of life. Therefore, there is no more condemnation because I am in Christ.*

Now partake of the cup of His blood. Remember that you have the legal right to come boldly into the Grace Court. Be confident in Christ as you face that old serpent, Satan, in court because your sins are already under the blood!

Decree Hebrews 4:16 out loud as you stand in front of the judge of all the earth:

> *Let us then fearlessly and confidently and boldly draw near to the throne of grace (the throne of God's unmerited favor to us sinners), that we may receive mercy [for our failures] and find grace to help in good time for every need [appropriate help and well-timed help, coming just when we need it].*

Now make this decree:

> Lord God, as I step into this Grace Court, I know that
> any remaining accusations, sins known and unknown (Ps.
> 19:12), and trespasses are covered by Your grace. Grace
> is free, unearned, and unmerited, so no matter what is
> going on in my life, I receive grace at no cost!
>
> In fact the Bible says You give grace to the humble,
> and because I have humbled myself to repent, even more
> grace is being released to me now in this court! I decree
> Matthew 5:4 over myself: "Blessed [forgiven, refreshed by
> God's grace] are those who mourn [over their sins and
> repent]" (AMP). Because I just grieved over my sin and
> repented, now I am being blessed, forgiven, and refreshed
> by Your grace!

Now decree these powerful grace scriptures and the matching
decrees over yourself while standing in the Grace Court. Craft
prayers out of each verse.

GRACE DECREES

> For it is by free grace (God's unmerited favor) that you
> are saved (delivered from judgment and made partakers
> of Christ's salvation) through [your] faith. And this [sal-
> vation] is not of yourselves [of your own doing, it came
> not through your own striving], but it is the gift of God.
> —EPHESIANS 2:8

> Lord God, Your free grace has totally delivered me from
> the unrighteous judgment the enemy filed against me
> in court. This happened not through my own works or
> striving but through the all-powerful work of Christ on
> the cross. Grace is the free gift of God, and I receive it,
> decree it, and believe it!

For sin shall not [any longer] exert dominion over you, since now you are not under Law [as slaves], but under grace [as subjects of God's favor and mercy].

—ROMANS 6:14

Lord, I decree that although I have sinned by breaking Your laws, sin no longer has dominion over me, because of grace. I decree that I am no longer a slave to a law I could never keep, but I am under grace as a subject of Your favor and mercy. I also decree that I will walk in the fruit of self-control, guided by the Spirit of life. I will not agree with temptation and sin but rather walk in the freedom of the Spirit's guidance in every issue.

But then Law came in, [only] to expand and increase the trespass [making it more apparent and exciting opposition]. But where sin increased and abounded, grace (God's unmerited favor) has surpassed it and increased the more and superabounded.

—ROMANS 5:20

Lord, I decree that every time I broke the law through idolatry, witchcraft, or any sins connected to serpents, Your grace increased and abounded, surpassed those sins, and increased the more and superabounded.

Now I declare to the enemy that my lawbreaking can no longer enable you to excite opposition against me. No matter how much my lawbreaking increased and expanded, grace has totally snuffed it out. Therefore, your military assaults released on me must immediately cease because of the power of grace and the cross to end the warfare.

[All] are justified and made upright and in right standing with God, freely and gratuitously by His grace (His unmerited favor and mercy), through the redemption which is [provided] in Christ Jesus.

—ROMANS 3:24

I decree that I have been totally vindicated of all charges in this court because the power of grace has made me justified and made me upright and in right standing with God. This is accomplished only through Jesus and not through my keeping of the law. I receive His unmerited favor and mercy over every area of my life right now.

[Therefore, I do not treat God's gracious gift as something of minor importance and defeat its very purpose]; I do not set aside and invalidate and frustrate and nullify the grace (unmerited favor) of God. For if justification (righteousness, acquittal from guilt) comes through [observing the ritual of] the Law, then Christ (the Messiah) died groundlessly and to no purpose and in vain. [His death was then wholly superfluous.]

—GALATIANS 2:21

As I stand in this Grace Court, before the throne and the judge's bench, I declare that I will never again treat God's gracious gift as something of minor importance and defeat its very purpose. I ask that the Holy Spirit always bring to my remembrance the importance of grace. Grace is what enables me to receive justification (righteousness, acquittal from guilt). This could never happen through my observing the ritual of the law. Therefore, I decree I will never again set aside and invalidate and frustrate and nullify the grace (unmerited favor) of God. If I do so, Christ would have died needlessly and to no purpose and in vain. "[His death was then wholly superfluous.]" I declare I will never neglect to remember grace so that I will never be severed from Christ again. Therefore, the serpent's attack on my life will be destroyed!

For you are becoming progressively acquainted with and recognizing more strongly and clearly the grace of our Lord Jesus Christ (His kindness, His gracious generosity,

His undeserved favor and spiritual blessing), [in] that
though He was [so very] rich, yet for your sakes He
became [so very] poor, in order that by His poverty you
might become enriched (abundantly supplied).

—2 CORINTHIANS 8:9

*I decree that through the counsel of the Holy Spirit, I will
grow in awareness and knowledge of Your endless grace. I
declare that I will become progressively more acquainted
with grace by studying Your Word and growing in grace
so that I will flourish in the courts of my God (Ps. 92:13).
I decree that Your grace will reveal to me Christ's kindness, gracious generosity, undeserved favor, and spiritual
blessing. Holy Spirit, show me more of the depths of grace.
I vow to search it out.*

COMMANDS

I command that my soul be healed by grace in Jesus' name.

I judge every idolatrous spirit and spirit of witchcraft.

I command all curses to break, in Jesus' name.

*I command fire to expose and drive out all serpents in
my life.*

*I command all serpents to unwind and go to the fiery abyss,
in Jesus' name.*

*I command all snake venom to come out of my body, in
Jesus' name.*

I command pain to go, in Jesus' name!

CHAPTER 5

SHAKING OFF VENOMOUS VIPERS THROUGH COMMUNION

*Is the cup of blessing which we bless [at the Lord's
Supper] not a sharing in the blood of Christ?
[Indeed it is.] Is the bread which we break not a
sharing in the body of Christ? [Indeed it is.]*
—1 CORINTHIANS 10:16, AMP

BECAUSE OF CHRIST we have one of the most potent anti-
venoms in our weapons arsenal: *Communion*. When we
partake of the Lord's Supper, we're instructed to do so in
remembrance of Him. What does that mean? When you participate in consuming His body and His blood, you're essentially com-
memorating and releasing what Jesus accomplished on the cross,
including the pivotal moment when He crushed the head of the
serpent.

Communion is an immensely effective antivenom—especially
when taken with remembrance! In 1 Corinthians 11:23–25 Paul

recounted the events of the last supper, when Jesus presented the bread and the cup for the disciples' consumption. As Paul expounded on that night, he reiterated that Jesus, numerous times, stated the need for us to partake of the elements with the power of remembrance:

> And when He had given thanks, He broke [it] and said, Take, eat. This is My body, which is broken for you. Do this to call Me [affectionately] to remembrance. Similarly when supper was ended, He took the cup also, saying, This cup is the new covenant [ratified and established] in My blood. Do this, as often as you drink [it], to call Me [affectionately] to remembrance.
> —1 CORINTHIANS 11:24–25

Notice Jesus repeatedly brings up the importance of remembrance. This means that as you partake, you would do well to deeply meditate on the Gospel accounts of the crucifixion and the truth of what Jesus accomplished for you when He trod on the serpent's head.

Many times I've seen people receive massive breakthroughs over snake attacks by just taking Communion several times a day, all the while speaking crucifixion verses against every serpent that is afflicting them. The crushing takes place in these moments as you soundly trample every enemy through the power of Jesus' body and blood.

When partaking of the elements, also remember that Jesus is the living Bread who came to bring life to the world. Thus, through the power of the supper, you can speak to your body of dirt, commanding it to vomit out the venom, toxins, and cancer the snake has injected into you, and then loose the life of Christ's body into every cell of your own.

TESTIMONY

Last year I had the privilege of praying for a man who had suffered numerous bouts with cancer. His health struggles spanned from lung cancer, then prostate cancer, and finally lymph node involvement around his neck, causing significant swelling. Moreover, his life had been marred by a series of traumatic events. When I asked him about his experiences, he recounted a litany of challenges, from personal trials to the complexities of dealing with church matters. Notably, he had served as a pastor, a role that often exposes individuals to a multitude of stressors and "sheep bites."

Unfortunately at first there was little movement or shrinkage from our intercession. So, I instructed him and his wife to soak in fire during the night to drive the serpent out of hiding. I told them I felt a serpent was carrying out a curse on them based on how much trauma he had experienced and the many times the disease had moved around. (When disease or pain moves around the body, it's often a sign of a serpent.)

They did as I instructed, and the next day on their way back to the meeting, he suddenly saw a serpent come out of his neck, then turn and look him right in the face! Fearlessly he followed the biblical mandate from Mark 16:18 to "take up serpents" (NKJV). He seized the serpent, tore it away, and cast it into the abyss while commanding it to burn and never return.

When the couple arrived at the meeting, my team and I went to work to now get the venom to expel from his body. I began to serve him multiple rounds of Communion, all the while decreeing we were doing this in remembrance of Jesus crushing the head of the serpent at the cross. As I kept feeding him the Bread of Life and the cup of the blood, I commanded his body of dirt to vomit out the toxin of the snake. At that, he fell under the power of God, and we laid him back on the floor.

As we stood observing him, suddenly it appeared as if he were choking. When we asked what was going on, he said large amounts of fluid that tasted something like chlorine were running down his throat, causing him to have to gulp down the liquid. The Communion was forcing the snake venom out of his body.

TRAUMA, SNAKES, AND COMMUNION

Did you know that trauma wounds the soul, then creates an opening for serpentine activity? Just as we discussed how sins, such as idolatry and witchcraft, create vulnerabilities that serpents exploit, trauma can also wound the soul and pave the way for these attacks.

What kinds of trauma are we talking about here? Well, it can involve any kind of prolonged stress, extended sickness, accidents, diseases, financial crises, family crises, marriage problems—essentially any type of difficult crisis or extreme stress. Especially repeated or prolonged trauma can create deep wounds within your soul. If left undealt with, these wounds can provide an opening for something in common with Satan, which allows him to exert his serpentine power over you.

As mentioned in John 14:30, our goal is to never have anything in common with the enemy, as this would give him power over us. Trauma-induced soul wounds can make this vulnerability possible.

THE SOUL-HEALING POWER OF COMMUNION

The good news is that Communion has the power to heal these wounds. Yes, you read that right—Communion can heal your soul. Let's turn to Matthew 26, where Jesus is serving Communion to His disciples.

> He {Jesus} took a cup, and when He had given thanks, He gave it to them, saying, Drink of it, all of you; for this is My blood of the new covenant, which [ratifies the agreement and] is being poured out for many for the forgiveness of sins.
>
> —MATTHEW 26:27–28

This passage is from the famous last supper, where Jesus takes the cup, gives thanks, and instructs His disciples to drink from it. The Greek word used for *drink* here is *pinō*, which means "to receive into the soul what serves to refresh, strengthen, nourish it unto eternal life."[1] Did you catch that? When you drink from the cup of His blood, you actually receive into your soul the power to be healed of every wound; to be refreshed, recharged, and reinvigorated in soul and body; to be nourished, reassured, and encouraged to continue running the race; and to be strengthened, braced, and fortified against future attacks.

This means that if you've experienced trauma that has left your soul weakened, leading to depression, oppression, discouragement, anxiety, fear, tormenting thoughts, or even difficulty making decisions, you can partake in Communion and be healed. Your soul will receive the deliverance it desperately needs through the power of His blood, effectively healing those wounds caused by traumatic incidents.

TRAUMA AND IDOLS

As you recall from chapter 1, idols, witchcraft, and serpents are like a demonic three-cord strand. When you make anything into an idol, you are inviting a witchcraft curse. Jezebel got her power from the idols she worshipped. Therefore, when you are in idolatry, you create something in common with witches. Then they can curse you, and the serpents carry out that curse.

What does this have to do with trauma? Whenever we are wounded by difficult trauma, our souls will reach out for something to bring them comfort and satisfaction. That often leads us to create idols in our lives, which we then rely on to bring comfort to our inner pain.

Have you ever noticed that when you are totally stressed out, you tend to eat more, even though you're not hungry? Do you binge-watch more TV or spend endless hours scrolling through your social media feeds when you're battling through a trial? Or perhaps you go to the mall, spending money you don't have, in an effort to "take a break" and release the pressure. Trauma, if left untreated, will lead to you creating idols in your life. Then the witches and serpents can have a heyday.

CHRIST DIED TO DEFEAT YOUR IDOLS

Conversely, did you know that one of the reasons Christ died was to heal you of idolatry? It's true! Check out this fabulous translation of Paul's words to the Corinthians:

> For if with his weak conscience and his fears and semi-belief in the beings he has so recently rejected, he return to their shrines and take a part in their feasts, is it not likely that this will have an influence upon his mind, and work on him to his own destruction? And so your clearer knowledge is likely to rob him of his chance to escape... *and so defeat the very purpose of Christ's death, which was to free our weak minds and souls and consciences from idols.*
> —1 CORINTHIANS 8:10–11, GWC, EMPHASIS ADDED

Notice the previous passage connects a weak soul with returning to worship at the shrines of idols you have already rejected. This proves that even though we have received salvation in Christ, we can be pulled back into the idolatry of the world—*when our souls become wounded.* However, as these verses so clearly state, the very purpose of Christ's death was to free your fragile soul from idols!

I know some people may think this is a stretch, but I believe the crown of thorns Jesus bore on the cross represented our idols. Consider the following verse:

> So now I declare that I will no longer drive out the people living in your land. *They will be thorns in your sides, and their gods will be a constant temptation to you.*
> —JUDGES 2:3, NLT, EMPHASIS ADDED

This was a warning to God's children that when they took possession of the Promised Land, they must continue to drive the pagan people out of their land and *refuse to worship their idols!* Those idols would become thorns in their sides. Unfortunately the people didn't listen, and eventually their idolatry resulted in their imprisonment in foreign nations and the loss of their inheritance in the land of milk and honey.

Thank God, Jesus wore the crown of thorns when He hung on that cross! His sacrifice empowers us to defeat every single idol that would try to ensnare our hearts.

Again, when you take Communion, you are doing it in remembrance of what He accomplished through Calvary. Through Communion your soul will be healed of trauma, becoming so strong that you won't want to run to idols for comfort. Look at what Jesus said in John 6, right before admonishing His followers to eat His flesh and drink His blood:

> Jesus said unto them, I am the bread of life: he that cometh to me shall never hunger; and he that believeth on me shall never thirst.
>
> —JOHN 6:35, KJV

The word *thirst* (Greek *dipsaō*), according to *Thayer's Greek-English Lexicon*, refers to "those...who painfully feel their want of, and eagerly long for, those things by which the soul is refreshed, supported, strengthened."[2] The danger of the wounded soul is that it is incessantly hungry and thirsty—for all the wrong things. Wounded people often find themselves going from one fix to the next in a futile effort to self-medicate their pain. They start feasting on idols of money and financial gain, excessive entertainment and enjoyment, and lusts and perversions, yet they are never able to quench their thirst. That is why each of us must run to Jesus and His table! He promises that when you do, you will never hunger and thirst again! His body and blood will cause your soul to be totally refreshed, supported, and strengthened in every place you need it.

SHIPWRECKS, TRAUMA, AND SERPENTS

Earlier I mentioned Paul's harrowing experience where, after a massive storm that culminated in a shipwreck, he was bitten by a poisonous viper on the island of Malta. Yet he shook the serpent off and was left unharmed (Acts 27:41–28:5). How did Paul manage to escape certain death from this snakebite, especially considering that his body and soul had just undergone the extreme trauma of the storm and its aftermath? As you will see, it's because he took Communion in the midst of it. Let's look at the events as they unfolded:

> Soon afterward a violent wind [of the character of a typhoon], called a northeaster, came bursting down from the island. And when the ship was caught and was unable to head against the wind, we gave up and, letting her drift, were borne along....They used supports with ropes to undergird and brace the ship; then afraid that they would be driven into the Syrtis [quicksands off the north coast of Africa], they lowered the gear (sails and ropes) and so were driven along. As we were being dangerously tossed about by the violence of the storm, the next day they began to throw the freight overboard; and the third day they threw out with their own hands the ship's equipment (the tackle and the furniture). And when neither sun nor stars were visible for many days and no small tempest kept raging about us, all hope of our being saved was finally abandoned....Then fearing that we might fall off [our course] onto rocks, they dropped four anchors from the stern and kept wishing for daybreak to come. And as the sailors were trying to escape [secretly] from the ship and were lowering the small boat into the sea, pretending that they were going to lay out anchors from the bow,

Paul said to the centurion and the soldiers, Unless these
men remain in the ship, you cannot be saved. Then the
soldiers cut away the ropes that held the small boat, and
let it fall and drift away.

—Acts 27:14–15, 17–20, 29–32

Do you see the extraordinary stress and trauma that Paul and
the people onboard had to endure? Have you ever faced a storm
that was so violent it felt like a typhoon? Did it burst on you unex-
pectedly, injecting a massive shock wave into every area of your
life? Was your storm so brutal that you lost all control and were
just borne helplessly along by the evil winds and the waves of the
crisis? Like these sailors, did you try to undergird yourself and
your family, business, church, or ministry with anything you could
get your hands on to keep from breaking apart? Did it seem like
everywhere you turned your feet were sinking in quicksand? Did
the waves get so violent that you had to throw all your freight
overboard, incurring major financial loss? Did you lose your ability
to get any rest, like Paul and those aboard, as they were forced
to throw all the furniture into the sea? Then when you didn't see
the light of day for what seemed like an eternity, did you give up
all hope of being saved? Maybe you even had close friends and
family members try to steal your lifeboat, then leave you alone on
a sinking ship.

If you answered yes to any or all of those questions, you are
undoubtedly wounded from the trauma of the storm and thus very
susceptible to the venom of a snakebite.

I know for sure Paul had been wounded by all the trauma he
experienced in his missionary journeys, including this shipwreck.
In 2 Corinthians 11, he wrote a list of his traumatic encounters,
including being persecuted, naked, hungry, stoned, beaten with
thirty-nine lashes five times, and shipwrecked three times, as well
as floating in the sea for a day and a night. Then at the end of the
list, he gave this revealing comment, which proves these traumas
indeed wounded him:

> If I must needs glory, I will glory of the things which con-
> cern mine *infirmities*.
>   —2 CORINTHIANS 11:30, KJV, EMPHASIS ADDED

The word *infirmities* (Greek *astheneia*) refers to "weakness, infirmity of the body...[and] of the soul."[3] This indicates that Paul knew these horrendous experiences had not just injured his physical body but also wounded his soul! Any rupture, opening, or fragmentation of your soul can allow a curse to alight and then a serpent to go to work for your destruction.

So, what did Paul do to be so healed of the traumatic effects of the shipwreck that he was impervious to the venom of that snake-bite? He took Communion in the middle of the storm.

COMMUNION IN THE STORM

Let me explain how I know that Paul partook of the lifesaving supper as the typhoon was raging. The Book of Acts tells the story:

> While they waited until it should become day, Paul entreated them all to take some food, saying, This is the fourteenth day that you have been continually in suspense and on the alert without food, having eaten nothing. So I urge (warn, exhort, encourage, advise) you to take some food [for your safety]—it will give you strength; for not a hair is to perish from the head of any one of you. Having said these words, he took bread and, giving thanks to God before them all, he broke it and began to eat. Then they all became more cheerful and were encouraged and took food themselves.
>   —ACTS 27:33–36

First Paul encouraged his fellow shipmates to eat some food to physically strengthen them after being in continual suspense for fourteen days. Then Paul partook of something much more nour-ishing than mere mortal fare; he ate of the supernatural power of

Christ Himself. In the middle of this deadly storm he took bread, gave thanks, broke it, then ate.

I know Paul was taking Communion because of the language the Scripture uses here. First the word *broke* (Greek *klaō*) is "used in the New Testament of the breaking of bread or communion."[4] And the word *bread* (Greek *artos*) refers to "the bread used at the love-feasts and at the Lord's Table."[5]

This absolutely shows that Paul took Communion amid the storm! When the wind was whipping at hurricane-force levels and the waves of the sea were violently tossing the boat around like a child's toy, Paul was eating the Bread of Life! Paul taught on Communion (1 Cor. 11). He understood its vast potency, the power it contained to strengthen, refresh, and nourish the soul during times of crises. It's precisely what he needed to receive healing in the face of such intense trauma during the storm and eventual shipwreck.

I believe this is the reason Paul was left unharmed by the deadly viper's bite. He had nothing in common with it! He had taken the Lord's Supper in remembrance of what his Savior, Jesus, did on the cross when He crushed the head of the serpent.

Notice that taking the Bread of Life also kept Paul's body in divine health, even after being bitten. Look at these verses:

> And he shook off the beast into the fire, and felt no harm. Howbeit they [the islanders] looked when he should have swollen, or fallen down dead suddenly: but after they had looked a great while, and saw no harm come to him, they changed their minds, and said that he was a god.
> —Acts 28:5–6, kjv

Swelling or inflammation comes on the body when a person is injured or ill in any way. Yet the bread of Communion caused Paul's body to reject and vomit out the venom! (I told you so!) The Lord's Supper kept his body in perfect homeostasis. The passage says he even sidestepped the effects of death itself!

REVIVAL HAPPENS ONCE YOU
HAVE BEEN DE-SNAKIFIED

After Paul was miraculously delivered from the venom of the serpent through the power of Communion, something fantastic took place:

> In the vicinity of that place there were estates belonging to the head man of the island, named Publius, who accepted and welcomed and entertained us with hearty hospitality for three days. And it happened that the father of Publius was sick in bed with recurring attacks of fever and dysentery; and Paul went to see him, and after praying and laying his hands on him, he healed him. After this had occurred, the other people on the island who had diseases also kept coming and were cured.
>
> —ACTS 28:7–9

After conquering that poisonous snake, Paul went on to spark a revival on the island! Once you get de-snakified, you won't have anything in common with demonic serpents either. Then you will be able to lay hands on all the snake-infested people on your "island" and see them healed as well. Revival will break out!

ACTIVATION

Now pause here and pray into this as you partake of Communion. I want you to begin by rereading the details of what happened to Paul during the storm. Meditate on them, and apply them to any circumstances you have experienced in your own storms. Then forgive the people involved in those traumatic experiences so you can begin receiving the power of Communion in your soul to refresh, strengthen, and nourish it.

Let's pray together:

> *Lord Jesus, before partaking of Your body and blood, I understand the importance of examining myself carefully.*

> *By judging the unforgiveness and bitterness in myself, I can avoid divine judgment* (1 Cor. 11:27–31). *So, right now I forgive those individuals involved in my trauma once and for all. I release any resentment or anger I have against them. I forgive them for any kind of betrayal and rejection, in Jesus' name.*
>
> *Furthermore, I decree that as I partake of the body and blood of Jesus, I am being healed of the shock of the sudden onset of the storm and the suspense and effects of the battle. I decree that my soul is being healed of losing hope during the storm, being stripped of my financial prosperity, and incurring loss of any kind. I also decree that the body and blood of Jesus are healing me of any weariness and burnout that came from the rest that was stolen from me during the storm. Lord, as I partake of Your body and blood, I affirm that my soul is being refreshed, nourished, and strengthened in my mind, will, and emotions. All the effects of trauma are being erased and eradicated in me. In Jesus' name, amen.*

As you consume the elements of Communion, worship for an extended period of time. Meditate on the fact that you are being refreshed, nourished, and strengthened in your soul, so there is no longer a common ground between you and the enemy, leaving the snake powerless over you. Then command your body, like Paul's body, to vomit out the venom of the serpent, and decree that every cell is being filled with life from the living bread of Christ.

COMMUNION STOPS THE BITE
OF THE FIERY SERPENT

Did you know that ancient Israel practiced Communion in the desert? They fed on the supernatural manna daily; it kept them healthy and whole during their forty-year journey. However, when they allowed themselves to become traumatized during the trip, they began to despise the living bread. They opened themselves up to serpent bites, and many of them died.

Before we begin this story, let's first establish through the New Testament that the Israelites did indeed partake in Communion in the desert. We find the proof here:

> I do not want you to be unaware, brothers, that our
> fathers were all under the cloud, and all passed through
> the sea, and all were baptized into Moses in the cloud and
> in the sea, and *all ate the same spiritual food, and all drank*
> *the same spiritual drink. For they drank from the spiritual*
> *Rock that followed them, and the Rock was Christ.*
> —1 CORINTHIANS 10:1–4, ESV, EMPHASIS ADDED

Let's ponder this "spiritual" food that they ate in the desert. It was the manna, the supernatural nourishment that descended for them from heaven every day. This manna was a representation of Christ's body, as Jesus declared:

> I assure you, most solemnly I tell you, Moses did not give
> you the Bread from heaven [what Moses gave you was not
> the Bread from heaven], but it is My Father Who gives
> you the true heavenly Bread….I [Myself] am this Living
> Bread that came down from heaven. If anyone eats of this
> Bread, he will live forever; and also the Bread that I shall
> give for the life of the world is My flesh (body).
> —JOHN 6:32, 51

Jesus is the living Bread that came down from heaven, both then and now. Here He reveals that the spiritual food consumed by the Israelites in the desert was, in essence, Himself. When they partook of the manna, it was a foreshadowing of the whole body of believers one day feasting on Christ, the living Bread who came to impart life to the world.

The Israelites also consumed "spiritual" drink in the desert. First Corinthians 10 says they drank from the Rock (capital *R*) and "the Rock was Christ" (v. 4, ESV). The spiritual drink they partook of was the water poured out from the Rock, symbolizing the blood of Jesus. You see, Moses struck the rock in the desert, and water poured out. Christ, the Rock, was struck on the cross, and blood poured out. When the people drank from the rock in the desert, they were prophetically drinking from what would become available to all God's children: the saving blood of Jesus Christ.

Just a note: This is why Moses was denied entry into the Promised Land after striking the Rock twice. Christ needed to be struck only once on the cross. He said, "It is finished"; thus, it was a onetime event that encompassed everything we need to totally overcome.

So, clearly the Israelites were participating in a precursor to Communion during their time in the desert. Why did God ordain this? Because the people had encountered extensive trauma during their journey, facing numerous challenges. God had to provide them with something supernatural to keep their souls nourished, refreshed, and strengthened.

And it worked. God promised that those who walked in obedience to His Word wouldn't suffer any of the diseases the Egyptians did (Exod. 15:26). I believe none of those who were faithful to God fell ill throughout their journey. And we know their garments didn't wear out in forty long years spent in the desert (Deut. 29:5). This was the work of the supernatural food and drink God so generously provided to keep them well and whole in every area.

When you don't take Communion, it opens you up to the bite of the serpent. Now let's return to 1 Corinthians 10. After Paul talks about the Israelites' partaking of Communion in the desert, he says something very interesting: "We should not test Christ, as some of them did—and were killed by snakes" (v. 9, NIV).

The people tested Christ in the desert by despising the manna, just when they needed it the most. Because of the stress and trauma of the journey they were getting wounded, which is exactly why God blessed them with the daily manifestation of the heavenly bread. It would refresh, nourish, and strengthen their souls when they needed it.

However, they let themselves be deeply affected by the trials and challenges of their desert journey, and then they chose instead to loathe the manna. What happened next? They were bitten by fiery serpents, and tragically many of them perished. Let's take a deeper look at the story:

> Then they journeyed from Mount Hor by the Way of the Red Sea, to go around the land of Edom; and the soul of the people became very discouraged on the way. And the people spoke against God and against Moses: "Why have you brought us up out of Egypt to die in the wilderness? For there is no food and no water, and our soul loathes this worthless bread." So the Lord sent fiery serpents among the people, and they bit the people; and many of the people of Israel died.
>
> —NUMBERS 21:4–6, NKJV

Did you catch that? First, the souls of the people became greatly discouraged. The Amplified Bible, Classic Edition words verse 4 in this manner: "The people became impatient (depressed, much discouraged), *because [of the trials] of the way*" (emphasis added). The trials and traumas the Israelites endured along the journey caused their souls to become wounded, and that is what allowed fiery serpents to bite them—and many of them died!

Notice that the people also began to sin out of those wounds. They got offended and let their mouths spew venom at Moses—and even God Himself.

A negative progression happens when you allow your soul to be wounded by trauma and don't take the necessary steps to get healed. You can fall into the trap of "talking smack," which then breaks a hole in your hedge of protection and allows a serpent in to bite you.

It's easy to fall into this snare, to get so hurt by the trials of life that you start complaining, then eventually become bitter and offended at people around you. If you get injured by negative circumstances, make sure you are on high alert to guard your heart—and your mouth. Otherwise you could find yourself in a full-on serpent assault.

The Israelites could have avoided being bitten by those fiery snakes by just eating the manna instead of loathing it. Look again at what they said to Moses: "There is no bread, and no water, *and our soul loathes this light bread*" (Num. 21:5, DARBY, emphasis added). Their wounded souls loathed the very thing God provided for them to stay whole. By embracing, appreciating, and understanding the gift of the heavenly bread God had provided for them, they would have been healed of the depression and discouragement that came on their souls from the trials of the way. The spiritual food would have nourished, refreshed, and strengthened them, healing the wounds that allowed the snakes to attack in the first place.

Remember, just as the Israelites loathed the manna and failed to recognize its significance, we also sometimes overlook the importance of taking Communion. Throughout Scripture the bread and drink represent Christ and His powerful provision, both before, during, and after His earthly life. It was through Communion that Paul overcame the traumas of the storm and the shipwreck. And I believe Communion kept the Israelites healthy in the desert until they chose to walk in disobedience to God. We must never forget the significance of this vital practice.

The Bible says, "The LORD sent fiery serpents among the people, and they bit the people; and many of the people of Israel died" (Num. 21:6, NKJV). I have often pondered why God would send serpents against His own people. I believe it's because by loathing the manna, they were ultimately loathing and rejecting His only begotten Son—the Bread of Life—who would suffer a horrible death on a cross so all could be saved.

GETTING RIGHT

Fortunately the people took the right steps to stop further loss of life from the deadly serpents. The first thing they did was repent.

> And the people came to Moses, and said, We have sinned,
> for we have spoken against the Lord and against you; pray
> to the Lord, that He may take away the serpents from us.
> So Moses prayed for the people.
> —NUMBERS 21:7

Some might say repentance is outdated, but it's not. If you're talking negatively about others, including complaining about God, your leaders, your spouse, or anyone else, you are opening yourself up to a snake attack. Repentance is your way out. Remember, "the venom of asps is beneath their lips. Their mouth is full of cursing and bitterness" (Rom. 3:13–14). In such moments it's crucial to repent promptly, because that's when the power of the cross is unleashed to crush the head of the serpent.

This, again, is why it was so vital that the people not let their souls loathe the supernatural food and drink. By continuing to partake with grateful hearts, they would release the crushing power of the cross against the snake attack. We must do the same.

The story continues, saying:

> And the Lord said to Moses, Make a fiery serpent [of
> bronze] and set it on a pole; and everyone who is bitten,
> when he looks at it, shall live. And Moses made a serpent of bronze and put it on a pole, and if a serpent had
> bitten any man, when he looked to the serpent of bronze
> [attentively, expectantly, with a steady and absorbing
> gaze], he lived.
> —NUMBERS 21:8–9

Why would God instruct Moses to craft a serpent and place it on a pole, telling the people to look at it to find healing and life? The answer lies in what this serpent represented: Christ Himself.

In John 3:14–15 Jesus said, "Just as Moses lifted up the [bronze] serpent in the desert [on a pole], so must the Son of Man be lifted up [on the cross], so that whoever believes will in Him have eternal life" (AMP).

That serpent on the pole was symbolic of Christ on the cross. But why would God use a serpent to represent the Savior of the world? Because on the cross Jesus went all the way back to the Garden of Eden, where the serpent first deceived Eve, to redeem all humankind from his wiles. It was on the cross that Jesus triumphed over that "old serpent," destroying his power forever. Therefore, when Moses crafted the bronze serpent and lifted it up on the pole, instructing the people to gaze at it intently, they were essentially being asked to look at the crucified Christ on the cross. The God-man, with arms stretched out, soundly trampled the serpent and gave us victory over the venom of the fiery snakes.

IF YOU WON'T EAT IT, YOU MUST BEHOLD IT

I must add that because the people had grown tired of eating the manna, God made them look at the bronze serpent—both of which were symbols of Jesus' body.

This is such a profound concept. They had grown weary of the manna. They had lost their taste for it and no longer desired to consume it. Thus, if the people wouldn't eat Him, God commanded them to look at Him. They were directed to gaze on the Bread of Life Himself, hanging on that pole—attentively, expectantly, with a steady and absorbing gaze. And in this way they would overcome the bites of the deadly vipers and live.

Can you imagine that day with all those venomous vipers slithering through the desert, claiming the lives of countless Israelites? *Yet by putting their full, uninterrupted attention on the One who would die for them, the people would live!* I can just see the deadly venom oozing out of the people's bodies as they continued to gaze on the symbol of the Savior on the cross, causing the serpents to be crushed.

ACTIVATION

Now prepare your Communion elements. As you do, I urge you to seek the Holy Spirit's guidance. Ask Him to show you where your soul has become "greatly discouraged" due to the trials of the way. Are you entangled in a fierce conflict or struggle? Is it related to your children's schooling? Or maybe it's an extremely difficult situation at work or church.

Maybe it involves a relationship with a friend or family member. Perhaps there is massive strife in your family or you're locked in a long, arduous conflict with your spouse. It's been years, and now your soul is weighed down by the burdens of this journey, and the way ahead appears discouraging.

Maybe you're caring for a family member battling a severe illness. You've been on a journey of faith, prayer, fasting, and seeking medical treatments, fervently believing for healing, decreeing, and warring for your loved one's recovery. You've tried numerous doctors, medications, and therapies, doing everything in your power to restore your family member's health. Despite the promises from the Lord you haven't witnessed the manifestation of healing, and your soul has become greatly discouraged due to the protracted struggle.

Perhaps you received a promise from God about a future spouse. You're not married yet, and you've held on to this promise for years. Along the way you've met multiple potential partners, only to see those relationships fall apart, leaving your heart broken each time. It seems like a series of disappointments, and your soul has grown increasingly discouraged.

Is it a financial struggle? Perhaps you've been striving to grow your business and take it to the next level, but despite your efforts it seems to be on a downward trajectory.

Is the trial related to your education? Have you experienced disappointments and setbacks in your educational journey, leaving you feeling disheartened? Have you found yourself progressing through life's challenges at a slower pace than you anticipated?

Whatever it is, let the Holy Spirit show you those issues that have left your soul greatly discouraged due to the obstacles you're encountering.

PARTAKE

As you prepare to partake of Communion, make sure to examine yourself as Paul admonished, for if you judge yourself, you will not face divine judgment. (See 1 Corinthians 11:28, 31, NKJV.)

If you are currently in the midst of a discouraging journey, you may have found yourself speaking negatively about individuals you've encountered along the way, expressing disdain for them and recounting their faults. If that is the case, let it go, forgive, and receive the cleansing blood of Jesus. Take a moment to drop to your knees as you do this; then speak these words:

> *Lord, I repent for speaking against other people and even You during the crises. I ask for Your forgiveness just as the Israelites repented for speaking against Moses and You. I do the same as I take steps toward my healing and deliverance from the venomous bite of the fiery serpent.*

While you are praying, worship the Lord with a powerful song because this is the moment for your healing. Now with the Communion elements in hand, pray with me as you partake of the Lord's Supper:

> *Lord God, as I come before You, I ask You to give me a deep revelation and understanding of the power of the heavenly manna, the living Bread, the Son of God, Jesus Christ. Then I will never take Communion for granted again. I won't let it fall to the wayside like the Israelites did. In every trial or trauma that I face, I will always remember that Christ's body and blood have been graciously supplied to me for my full healing. Amid every storm, every crisis, every challenge, every disappointment, I will run to His table to taste and see that the Lord is good!*

Now, Lord, I recognize that I've grown depressed and discouraged because of the trials of the way. As I've traversed this desert, I've encountered numerous attacks, crises, and stressful events. Yet even though I've been totally overtaken by the challenges of my life, I know that You have provided me with the healing perfection of Christ—His sacrificed body and His poured-out blood.

I thank the Lord Jesus Christ for being the serpent on the pole. On the cross Jesus redeemed me from everything that was lost in the garden to the serpent. So now I give You the adoration You deserve by looking on You attentively, expectantly, and with a steady and absorbing gaze, and I know that as I do, I will live! I believe as I partake of Your body, the serpent's venom will be pushed all the way out of my physical body.

Lord Jesus, I worship, honor, and celebrate You for giving me the cup of Your blood, which causes my soul to be nourished, refreshed, and strengthened. I decree that when I drink the cup of Your blood, my mind is healed of tormenting thoughts, my will is freed from any wounds that are controlling my decisions, and my emotions are healed and controlled by the Holy Spirit. I declare that Your blood sustains, encourages, reinvigorates, revitalizes, supports, reinforces, and fortifies my soul. I decree that the blood is causing me to be totally healed of trauma.

Now before you partake of the elements, remember that whoever gazed at the serpent on the pole—expectantly, attentively, and with an absorbed focus—would live. Hold up the body of Christ, the living Bread who came down from heaven, and in your sanctified imagination, see Christ. Look at Him with expectation, attentiveness, and absorption. Put aside any distractions, and focus intently on Christ. See Him lifted up, carrying all the sin that originated from the serpent, all the way back to the Garden of Eden. See Him lifting your sin from you as it is imputed to Him and His righteousness is imputed back to you. Keep your focus on Christ, recognizing how good He is. He is far above the snake line. See Him lifted up, see Him dying, and then see Him being resurrected for you. Visualize Him ascending into heaven, completely victorious, then seated next to God, and know that you are seated next to Him, being in Him.

Take a moment to dwell on these truths. See where you are in the spiritual realm, seated in heavenly realms with Christ by virtue of your being in Him. Because of Him you are no longer under the enemy's influence. You are healed because of Christ. You are delivered because of Him. Continue to gaze at Him in His glory. He is majestic, glorified, the King of kings, the Lord of lords.

He is your Savior, your Redeemer, the Lover of your soul, and the majestic King. He is awesome. He is a beautiful Savior, a spring of living water, and our Redeemer. He is the Alpha and Omega, the Beginning and the End, the crusher of the serpent, the victor through the cross. He is our perfect sacrifice, the Lamb without spot or blemish. None can open the scroll in heaven but Him!

Stay in this moment, and thank Him. Praise Him. Worship Him. Give Him honor and glory. Lift Him up. Magnify His name.

Now partake of the bread of Communion, and as you do, pray with me:

> Lord Jesus, I thank You that as I partake of Your body, I do it in remembrance of You and all that You achieved on the cross for me when You crushed the head of the serpent. As I partake of Your body, I declare it will force the venom of the serpent out of my body of dirt and impart Your life to every place where the serpent bit and wounded my body of dirt, destroying my organs, bones, joints, skin, eyes, and ears and every other part of me. In every place where the venomous, demonic snake sought to inflict sickness and disease, I receive Your life now.

Next take the cup and say this:

> *This is the cup of Jesus' blood, poured out for the remission of sins. As I stand in this court, testifying to the power of the blood of Jesus to conquer the enemy on my behalf and cleanse me from my sins, I believe that the record of accusations filed against me in this court is being completely removed, completely washed away. I receive the power of His blood, which He shed on the cross, and the crushing of the serpent's head now, in Jesus' name. I declare to every serpent attacking me that it must let go because of Jesus' victory on the cross, where He destroyed every work of the enemy. In Jesus' name, amen.*

Then speak these commands:

> *In the name of Jesus I command trauma to leave now. I curse it at its core, rendering it unable to produce any further harm. I take every serpent to court and render it powerless by court decree and the name of Jesus.*
>
> *I command the venom of the serpent to be expelled from my body as the Bread of Life, the living Bread, flows through my entire being to mend, restore, and rejuvenate me right now in the name of Jesus. Father, I thank You. The serpent can no longer bite me because of what Christ achieved for me when He crushed the serpent's head on the cross.*
>
> *Now I decree that I will live! I command life to flow into my body, finances, ministry, business, family, marriage, relationships, children, and every other aspect of my life. In Jesus' name, amen.*

CHAPTER 6

LEVIATHAN: THE KING OF THE CHILDREN OF PRIDE

In that day [the Lord will deliver Israel from her ene-
mies and also from the rebel powers of evil and dark-
ness] His sharp and unrelenting, great, and strong sword
will visit and punish Leviathan the swiftly fleeing ser-
pent, Leviathan, the twisting and winding serpent.
—ISAIAH 27:1

THE NAME LEVIATHAN, as used in Scripture, refers to "a wreathed animal, i.e. a serpent (especially the crocodile or some other large sea-monster); figuratively, the constellation of the dragon; also as a symbol of Babylon."[1]

This makes Leviathan a shape-shifting entity that can appear as a dragon (Ps. 74:13–14), a crocodile (Job 41:1), or a serpent (Isa. 27:1). This is important to know so that when you see him in his many forms, you will know whom you are dealing with.

I've witnessed Leviathan appearing in varying ways. Once, he looked like a sea monster but with a serpent's tail and a dragon's head. When you observe Leviathan associated with oceans, it symbolizes his control over masses of people, continents, and the world at large.

On another occasion I observed him as a crocodile hidden in the muddy banks of a river. In this vision the crocodile's obscurity in the mud was analogous to his secret control in the banking system and even in our own personal finances.

Many other times I have seen waters full of alligators that would try to attack people when they ventured too close or became careless around them. Each time I saw this, I knew Leviathan was on assignment against God's people, and it was vital for the body of Christ to understand how to properly engage this powerful principality.

Recognizing Leviathan's appearances in various forms can guide your strategy to confront him effectively. For now let's look at this description of him in Isaiah:

> In that day [the Lord will deliver Israel from her enemies and also from the rebel powers of evil and darkness] His sharp and unrelenting, great, and strong sword will visit and punish Leviathan the swiftly fleeing serpent, Leviathan the twisting and winding serpent.
>
> —ISAIAH 27:1

This scripture reveals that Leviathan will often appear as a serpent, and one of his main tactics is to twist people's conversations. He creates swirls and confusions in emails, texts, and any kind of communication. When the Bible refers to him as a "swiftly fleeing...twisting and winding serpent," it isn't implying that he runs away from you. Rather, it is describing how he moves in a snakelike fashion, darting between people as they converse. As he slithers back and forth, he distorts their words and their intended meanings. Unfortunately, when someone expresses a thought, the others interpret it differently, leading to misunderstandings and, frequently, disputes. This causes everyone involved to be unable to reach an agreement, all the while accusing one another of making statements they never uttered. In some cases an individual heavily influenced by Leviathan may even deny saying things he or she clearly stated in front of numerous people, causing confusion and conflict among those who witnessed the conversation.

I recently experienced a situation involving someone I deeply care about. They had detailed conversations with several people, including myself, about some very important business matters. Later, however, they denied saying anything of the sort, despite the fact that four or five witnesses had heard them. When confronted, they accused me of misinterpreting their words. That is when I reminded them that every matter is established by the testimony of two or three witnesses (Matt. 18:16) and that I had those testimonies.

This person finally admitted that similar incidents had occurred in their life before. However, even in that admission, Leviathan was still twisting the facts. They said other people in the past had made the same accusations against them, then proceeded to say those claims were false. My reply was, "Unfortunately you are the common denominator in all these conflicts."

When you encounter such situations, it's a clear indicator of Leviathan's presence. Leviathan's twisting extends far and wide, causing havoc and chaos such as marital discord, ministry shipwrecks, church divisions, business troubles, and more in our lives.

Leviathan is a troublemaker who manipulates individuals, stirs up turmoil, and distorts truths. It's crucial that we recognize his activities; that's why Job 41:31 says, "He makes the deep boil like a pot; he makes the sea like a [foaming] pot of ointment."

Consider the symbolism here: the sea represents the masses, the oceans of people. Leviathan is a pot stirrer, for sure, agitating and causing turmoil among people everywhere. He is one of the powers behind the state of the world today, which is full of anger, bitterness, and confusion, where strife permeates every corner.

The oceans of humanity are foaming at the mouth, overflowing with anger and vitriol, a phenomenon seen online, on television, in politics, and throughout society. Leviathan, the pot stirrer, is the driving force behind this chaos. He twists people's words and distorts the moral compass and scriptural values of nations. As a principality he exerts his influence over not just individuals but entire continents and across the world's seven mountains.

LEVIATHAN AND THE BRIARS AND THORNS IN YOUR SOUL

Leviathan is intimately connected to the soul, through which he can govern the people of the nations. We saw proof of this in Isaiah 27:1, which gives us not only a description of Leviathan but also a declaration that God Himself will fight against this demonic principality and slay him with "His sharp and unrelenting, great, and strong sword."

Then the chapter takes on a totally different tone. This is where we see the connection between this twisting serpent and the soul.

> In that day [it will be said of the redeemed nation of Israel], A vineyard beloved and lovely; sing a responsive song to it and about it! I, the Lord, am its Keeper; I water it every moment; lest anyone harm it, I guard and keep it night and day. Wrath is not in Me. Would that the briers and thorns [the wicked internal foe] were lined up against Me in battle! I would stride in against them; I would burn them up together.
>
> —ISAIAH 27:2–4

What's going on here? Isaiah went from describing God's punishment of Leviathan to comparing Israel to a beloved and lovely vineyard. Why? Here the Lord declares Himself as the Keeper of the vineyard, diligently watering it every morning to prevent any harm. His protection is so great that it extends day and night.

God is proclaiming His unending, tireless love and devotion for us, the members of His beautiful vineyard. However, every vineyard can grow briars and thorns, as the previous verses state, if it is not well tended. This is where the connection between Leviathan and your soul comes in.

Vineyards can lose their fruitfulness if briars and thorns are allowed to grow in them, choking out the harvest. We are God's vineyard, and regrettably we often have these thorny, prickly plants growing. Notice that God calls them "the wicked internal foe." What does this mean? The briars and thorns represent the chaff in your soul, the junk in your trunk, which allows the serpents to gain legal access to your life.

It is "the wicked internal foe" that resists God. The thorns and briars in our souls fight against the Lord and His purposes for our lives, and they also break a hole in God's hedges so a serpent can come in and bite us. I love how the Lord says He wants to stride in against those briars and thorns and burn them up together! This concept is reminiscent of what John the Baptist prophesied to the Pharisees about the One who would come to baptize them with the Holy Spirit and fire. The burning Savior would separate the chaff from the wheat and burn up that chaff with unquenchable fire (Matt. 3:11–12).

Don't forget that the fire in the Upper Room "diffused throughout their souls" (Acts 2:4). Its purpose was to consume the wicked internal foe within the disciples. This divine fire transformed Peter from the man who had denied Jesus and retreated from ministry into the bold preacher who led three thousand people to salvation. Obviously the fire had purged the briars and thorns from Peter's vineyard.

That same Holy Ghost fire will burn up the wicked internal foe in your own mind, will, and emotions that you have in common with Leviathan. Isaiah started the chapter with a judgment against Leviathan, letting us know that God will take care of him with His sharp, unrelenting sword. Nevertheless, your responsibility is to receive the baptism of fire so the wicked internal foe in your garden will burn! Then you will have nothing in you that's in common with Leviathan.[2]

PRIDE—THE WICKED INTERNAL FOE

Now let's delve into some of the briars and thorns in your vineyard (your soul) that you have in common with Leviathan. In this chapter we will address the issue of pride. Job 41:34 in the King James Version refers to this demonic serpent as the "king over all the children of pride." This signifies that Leviathan rules over individuals who harbor pride in their hearts. Just as a king reigns over his servants, Leviathan exercises full control over those consumed by pride.

Interestingly enough, Job 41 also says that Leviathan's scales are his pride:

> His scales are [the crocodile's] pride, [for his back is made of rows of shields] shut up together [as with] a tight seal; one is so near to another that no air can come between them. They are joined one to another; they stick together so that they cannot be separated.
>
> —JOB 41:15–17

Leviathan's scales are a source of his pride because they are like an impenetrable row of shields. If you are operating in pride, then you have something in common with Leviathan, making it impossible for you to penetrate his armor. These scales, akin to pride, shield him from all forms of attack, be it from a javelin, a sword, or any other weapon. Pride acts as an impermeable barrier, enabling his demonic control over your life to continue.

If you want to break free from his control, you must humble yourself. Have you ever encountered someone whose pride is as impassable as these scales? No matter what you say or do, the person remains obstinate and unyielding. Don't forget the biblical admonishment, "Pride goes before destruction, and a haughty spirit before a fall" (Prov. 16:18). This verse underscores the destructive consequences of pride and its role in causing the downfall of individuals who do not humble themselves.

Marriages in particular are vulnerable to the devastating effects of pride, as both parties often believe they are in the right, leading to discord and separation. Perhaps you and your spouse find it challenging to communicate. Conversations become a frustrating cycle of misunderstanding and obstinacy. One says, "You said this," and the other denies it, leading to more confusion. Or maybe one of the spouses wants things done a specific way while the other utterly disagrees. It becomes a never-ending back-and-forth, marked by stubbornness and pride, and guess who's lurking in the background? Leviathan.

I'm not one to hold back, so let me share a personal anecdote. My husband and I, married for nearly two decades, have had our fair share of conflicts. We've weathered massive storms that could've driven us apart. But what's kept us together is the recognition that Leviathan is often the instigator behind our disputes.

Countless times we've found ourselves in heated arguments, unable to see eye to eye or even offer an apology. In the middle of those impasses God would remind me, "Leviathan is at work here. He's twisting your words, stirring the pot, and causing unnecessary strife. Repent of pride, and break your agreement with him; then judge the altar of pride within you and your husband."

So, in the midst of these *Clash of the Titans* moments, I would step aside and engage in worship instead of letting the conflict escalate. I would humbly repent of pride, for myself and my husband; then, acknowledging our commonality with Leviathan, I would judge the altar of pride in our souls. Next I'd bring the matter to the court of heaven, using my exousia authority—the power of judicial decisions—to judge Leviathan's activity. I don't cast him out or rebuke him; I rely on the highest court in the universe to arrest him and restrain his influence in Jesus' name.

Remarkably, within just a few minutes, my husband would often return from his space, apologizing and seeking to make amends. I always responded in kind, expressing my love, and then everything would shift—almost instantly. I've lost count of how many times this has happened in our life. It's kept our marriage together. You too can apply this approach to your marriage and overcome the challenges you face when Leviathan is operating in the background.

In the next chapter I will show you through proof in the Bible that you have the legal right to take Leviathan to court.

RID YOURSELF OF THE LANDING STRIP OF PRIDE

As we go into this activation to remove pride, prepare as many servings of Communion as you can and have them ready to partake of. As you will see in future chapters, this Leviathan spirit also causes cancer and diseases of all kinds, so you must really press into getting healed and delivered of every area in your life that is in common with him.

Take note that as you go after pride, you may begin to experience certain manifestations, even including what I call a "Leviathan headache." This pain, wrapped around your head, especially in the frontal lobe, is a sign that Leviathan is on you. Even though he will try to resist as you break free, you will have the final victory because of Christ.

Additionally you may feel a swirling sensation in your breasts and private areas. This relates to the curses Leviathan inflicts on the breasts and womb, which we will discuss further based on Job 3. As I mentioned before, I have felt swirling in my breasts when serpents came out. I remember one event in Minnesota where I taught extensively on Leviathan and pride. At the end of the teaching time, as we all went into Communion, I felt it again. I knew that devil had found his way back in due to my own pride. I worshipped and then took Communion with the rest of the people attending the event. Then the next day something amazing happened.

As I was getting ready, I saw what appeared to be a huge boil on one of my breasts. I got in the shower and, under the hot water, pressed on it a bit. Immediately a huge stream of gray gunk came out! It was gross, to say the least, but I was ecstatic! I knew I had been delivered of another round of potential cancer brought on by this beast. And because he was now evacuated, my body could expel that toxin through the power of Communion!

Lastly you might experience a sensation of constriction around your neck or movement in your physical body. This is a manifestation of the presence of Leviathan, python, and other serpents carrying out a curse on your physical body. Keep worshiping in fire and taking Communion to drive them out.

SYMPTOMS OF PRIDE

As you go through this list of pride symptoms, pause and take Communion whenever something hits home for you.

One common symptom is that you take excessive pride in personal achievements, such as a history of past jobs or educational accomplishments. I remember a beloved member of our staff who possessed impressive educational qualifications and a wealth of skills. This individual was undoubtedly anointed. However, it became apparent that they relied heavily on their education and took an immense sense of pride in it. Unfortunately this allowed Leviathan to twist conversations, create misunderstandings, and sow discord within our ministry.

Note: If you find yourself harboring resentment toward your business or company, perhaps because you have impressive qualifications or feel like you should be earning more, it's essential to check your heart. While your educational achievements might indeed warrant a higher income, allowing pride and resentment to take root can open the door to Leviathan's influence.

If this resonates with you, take a moment to repent. Say this:

> *Lord Jesus, I examine my heart now and judge myself, lest I face divine judgment. I repent for any excessive pride I've taken in my accomplishments and education. I am thankful for the knowledge You've granted me, and I desire to use it for the Holy Spirit and for the kingdom's*

work. However, I will not allow pride to rule over me, for
Leviathan is the king of the children of pride.

Speak these words and then partake of the Communion elements, believing that God is cleansing you from the effects of
pride with the Bread of Life and His precious cup. Remember that
drinking from the cup nourishes, refreshes, and strengthens your
soul. Drink, and thank the Lord for His presence.

Now let's address another symptom of pride: the need to have
the last word. I can relate to this one personally. In arguments with
my husband I used to insist on having the final say, even to the
point of shouting it out as I left the room, then slamming the door
behind me.

If you identify with this behavior, repentance is in order. Join
me in saying this prayer:

> *Lord, the compulsion to have the last word is a sign of*
> *pride. It reveals that I believe my words are more impor-*
> *tant than anyone else's, and I acknowledge that this atti-*
> *tude places me above others. I desire humility that leads to*
> *exaltation, as pride brings only destruction and a hard fall.*
> *Lord, heal me of this need to have the last word. I repent*
> *of my pride and decree that through the cross, I have been*
> *acquitted of all charges the devil has made against me.*
> *Because of Your grace I am in right standing with You, in*
> *Jesus' name. Amen.*

Now partake once more. Remember, as you take Communion,
you can also intercede for others who exhibit these prideful symptoms, including your spouse. While examining yourself, you can
simultaneously pray for their deliverance and transformation.

> *Lord, as I relinquish my pride, I ask that You move in*
> *the hearts of my family members, my spouse, my coworkers,*
> *my friends, and my ministry partners. I decree that pride*
> *has no place in our relationships, and I ask that You strike*

down any influence of Leviathan in our communication
and interactions. In Jesus' name, amen.

Another common symptom of pride is when individuals consistently redirect conversations back to themselves. You've likely encountered this scenario. You call someone to touch base, and immediately they launch into a monologue about themselves—what they're going through, what they need—without ever inquiring about your well-being. Or perhaps they'll ask, "How are you?" as an afterthought, only to interrupt when you start sharing. Then they redirect the conversation back to themselves again. It can also happen in a setting where many people are gathered and one person dominates the discussion, talking about his or her own needs, experiences, and accomplishments with little regard for others.

I've consciously made an effort to break this pattern in my own life. For example, when I'm dining with others, I initiate conversations that allow each person at the table to share experiences and stories. I'll ask, "What's going on with you?" and let the person speak, showing interest in his or her life. Then I will gently guide the conversation to the next person until everyone has had an opportunity to share. This practice helps build camaraderie and fosters a deeper appreciation for each person in the team or group.

If you recognize that you're the one monopolizing conversations, it's essential to take a step back and let others have their turns. Pass the metaphorical football so they can share their thoughts and experiences. Otherwise individuals driven by pride, controlled by Leviathan, will continue to dominate discussions, leaving everyone else feeling unsatisfied.

Let's pray these words together:

Lord Jesus, I repent for the times I've made myself the center
of attention without realizing I am under the influence of
Leviathan, the ruler of the children of pride. Lord, help
me show deference to others in conversation and conduct so
they know they are valued. I also repent on behalf of those

I know who constantly exhibit this behavior. Lord, I decree
that the altars of pride and self-centeredness within me and
within them will be completely destroyed by a judgment
from this heavenly court. In Jesus' name, amen.

Now partake of the elements of Communion.

Thank You, Lord, for binding the Leviathan spirit in me
and in others that compels us to talk only about ourselves
without concern for the others around us. I decree that
this predilection toward selfishness is bound by Your work
on the cross. I release the fruit of the Spirit into my life as
I walk out Your love and grace toward those whom You
place in my path. In Jesus' name, amen.

Another symptom of pride is the belief that one is always right.
This is a challenging mindset to root out. I'm sure you've encountered people like this, and perhaps you've been one of them at
times. I once had a cupholder on my desk with a message that
humorously claimed, "I always take advice from myself because I'm
always right." Even though this sentiment can be amusing, it highlights a common tendency in many of us—to never admit we are
wrong, whether to others or to ourselves.

We need to pause and reflect on this inclination. While you may
possess valuable wisdom on various matters, no one is infallible,
being right 100 percent of the time. It's crucial to take a step back,
listen to different perspectives, evaluate them, and seek guidance
from the Holy Spirit. Sometimes you'll be right, and sometimes
you'll be dead wrong. Therefore, refrain from staunchly defending
any positions that you haven't first confirmed with the Holy Spirit.

Just a note: I will always stand my ground when, first, I'm certain I've heard from God and, second, a multitude of counselors
have borne witness to that word of God being true in my life
(Prov. 11:14). However, if I'm merely expressing *my* own thoughts
and ideas without a very clear word from God, I try to pause and
reassess, recognizing that unchecked pride might be at play.

Are you ready to address this issue? Let's pray together:

> *Lord Jesus, I repent for thinking I have all the answers—because I don't. Together, as a team, with my spouse, family, friends, leaders, employers, coworkers, and church, I have access to all the wisdom I need through the Holy Spirit. Lord, I want to create space for others to express themselves. I judge any inclination within me that believes my opinion is the only valid one and that I can trust only myself, while distrusting others. I also judge anything in others that prevents them from offering opinions guided only by the Holy Spirit. Let their contributions be valid because they come from the Spirit of God, just as mine can be too. Lead me exclusively by the Holy Spirit and not by the pride lurking within my soul. In Jesus' name, amen.*

Now partake of the Communion elements.

> *I decree that I speak only from the Holy Spirit's guidance and not of my own selfish pride. I openly seek the opinions and wise counsel of others who know You and who seek Your face. I welcome Your guidance in my life—through Your Word and through the wisdom that comes from other servants of Yours who speak truth into my life. Through the cross I have been acquitted of all charges the devil has made against me, and I decree that I am in right standing with You because of Your grace. Thank You, Lord. Amen.*

Let's turn to some other symptoms of pride and the influence of Leviathan: mocking leadership and other people, rolling one's eyes in disdain, and engaging in gossip about others. I once had an employee who showed this kind of disdain for me and others. (Later, it was revealed she was dependent on opiate pain medication.) One day during our collaborative work on a media project, we had a disagreement about the direction the project should take. Suddenly she rolled her eyes at me while brazenly stating, "I have to take a pill to be able to work with you every day." This type of behavior represents disrespect and dishonor, embodying the spirit of mockery, as well as rebellion against leadership. Rolling one's eyes signifies disrespect and conveys a message akin to *You're so foolish*. It's a form of mockery that's utterly disrespectful.

Back in the day, on the streets, anyone who rolled their eyes at me quickly learned not to do it again. But I've been transformed more into Christ's image by the Spirit since then, and I no longer respond violently to disrespect. Instead, I prefer to go low in the Lord and take my position in the spiritual court to address this behavior.

The serpentine spirit attempts to degrade, mock, dismiss, and show disrespect and dishonor toward leadership, peers, or anyone with whom it's associated. You might have come across numerous online platforms dedicated to criticizing and ridiculing individuals, including me, for our doctrinal beliefs. The source behind these sites is often a twisting brood of vipers influencing the people. They spread venomous remarks and malicious intent much like the religious Pharisees I mentioned earlier who were under the serpents' control.

Have you been engaging in mocking or gossiping about others, including leaders of churches, businesses, or any other organizations? Let's take a moment to repent together. As you hold the bread and the cup, declare these words out loud:

> *Lord God, I pledge not to engage in mockery, twisting, or dishonor because I understand it opens the door to demonic influence in my life. I ask the Holy Spirit to continually remind me to remain humble, for You exalt the humble and bring low the proud in spirit. Thank You, God, for cleansing me of this sin. I renounce rolling my eyes at people or making derogatory gestures and remarks, because I desire to honor others. I believe that when I show honor, I will receive honor in return, even if it's undeserved. In Jesus' name, amen.*

Take Communion now.

Lord Jesus, I decree that I walk in a spirit of honor—toward You and toward those who serve You. I do not allow Leviathan a foothold in my life due to my pride as demonstrated through any mockery, dishonor, or disrespect of the authorities You have placed in my life. I decree that through the cross I have been acquitted of all charges the enemy has made against me, and I am in right standing with You because of Your grace. In Jesus' name, amen.

Here is another symptom of pride: You often struggle to accept constructive criticism. Pride prevents you from easily admitting you are wrong. Receiving criticism, even if it's intended to be helpful, can be challenging for anyone. It can sometimes make people feel abandoned, rejected, or ashamed, as if they have done something wrong. Yet we all make mistakes, and it's essential to be open to constructive criticism, ideally delivered with love rather than as a harsh blow.

We must approach situations like this with prayer. When someone offers feedback that feels critical, even if we initially feel too wounded or defensive to accept or discuss it, we can respond by saying, "I truly value your input. May I take some time to pray about it?" Then, we should take that moment to seek guidance from the Holy Spirit. By doing so, we can gain insight from the Holy Spirit's perspective. God may reveal that some aspects of the feedback are true.

If you're offered constructive feedback, avoid an immediate knee-jerk reaction of dismissal, as there may be revelations that can set you free, help you grow, cause you to prosper, expand your understanding, and shed the limitations holding you back. It's vital to pray and reflect on constructive criticism rather than immediately rejecting it.

A related issue is that of being unteachable. If you're not open to learning and growth, you'll struggle to advance in your administrative skills, your leadership abilities, and the prosperity of your family, ministry, or business. Remaining unteachable will keep you stagnant, hindering your progress in various aspects of life. Many times success depends on your willingness to receive feedback, even if it's challenging, and then learn from it.

So, let's pray for the ability to receive constructive criticism and be teachable:

> *Lord, I desire to be teachable. I want to accept constructive criticism that comes from the Father and the Holy Spirit, both through Your Word and through other people. I commit to learning and growing. I decree this in the name of Jesus, for the sake of my family's prosperity, health, and happiness, as well as for the growth of my ministries, businesses, and endeavors. Grant me a teachable and humble spirit right now. In Jesus' name, amen.*

Now partake of the Communion elements.

> *Father, I thank You that through the cross I have been acquitted of all charges the devil has made against me, and I am in right standing with You because of Your grace. I decree right now that I have a humble and teachable spirit, open to Your direction, whether that comes from Your Word, through the prompting of Your Spirit, or through the constructive criticism of those people You have put into my life. I will not be offended when areas of improvement are pointed out to me, but I commit to grow in the Spirit, becoming more and more like Your precious Son, Jesus. In His name, amen.*

Here are a few more points to consider. People in pride often love being served but resist serving others. They may feel too important to engage in mundane tasks or believe they should be exempt from such responsibilities. This attitude can also be found in employees who refuse to perform certain tasks because they consider that work beneath them. However, it's important to remember that everyone, regardless of position, should be willing to perform all tasks, even if they seem mundane.

Daily I perform numerous tasks I do not necessarily enjoy, but they are essential. Serving others, even in small ways, is an important aspect of humility. I recall that during one of David Herzog's stadium meetings, I offered to help serve in any capacity, even if it meant cleaning bathrooms and maintaining the facilities throughout the event. I expressed my willingness to pray for the sick among the crowd without needing a spot on the stage. This attitude of servanthood is what defines us, and it is part of why people appreciate our ministry.

I've witnessed individuals entering the ministry solely seeking to acquire an anointing and secure a spot onstage. However, it doesn't work that way. True anointing comes from a secret place of prayer and communion with God. My personal philosophy is simple: if it means scrubbing toilets to serve others and further God's work on the earth, then so be it.

So, if you've ever exhibited a resistance to this type of service, repent and ask for a heart that's open to serving others willingly. Say this:

> Lord God, grant me humility. Help me willingly engage in tasks I might not want to do because they are inconvenient, challenging, or dirty. Forgive me, Lord, and cleanse me of the belief that I am above certain responsibilities. Thank You for removing this demonic altar and the power of the serpent from my life, enabling me to walk in humility and grace. I am ready to do whatever it takes, so reveal to me what You would have me to do. I know, Lord, that You will exalt me at the right time.

Speak these words:

> I also condemn the altar within me that seeks only the company of prominent individuals. I condemn the altar

that yearns only for the spotlight and is unwilling to serve God's kingdom in humility. I pass judgment on that altar right now in the name of Jesus.

Now partake of the Communion elements.

Father, I decree that through the cross I have been acquitted of all charges the devil has made against me, and I am in right standing with You because of Your grace. I decree, heavenly Father, that I have a spirit of humility and willingness to serve You in any capacity in Your kingdom. As Your Word declares, the last shall be first, and the first shall be last. I only want to serve You in any way that I can. In Jesus' name, amen.

Now put on some worship music (I recommend Mercy Culture), and enter fiery worship to burn up the wicked internal foe in your soul and drive Leviathan out of your life! Then say this prayer:

Lord God, in Jesus' name, I step into the court of the Ancient of Days. I ask that the court be convened and the books be opened as the Ancient of Days takes His seat. I pray that the power of this beast, as described in Daniel 7, be stripped away. During the hearing of this court case, I ask that streams of fire emanate from the judge's bench and consume the wicked internal foe, the thorns and briars within my vineyard. I pray that this baptism of fire from the Holy Spirit will separate the chaff of pride from the wheat within me and burn it up with unquenchable fire. I decree that through the cross, I have been acquitted of all charges the enemy has made against me, and I am in right standing with You because of Your grace. In Jesus' name, amen.

Then add this:

Lord, because of the exousia authority You have given me to release judicial decisions against any serpent and over all the power of the enemy, in the court of heaven I now judge the spirit of Leviathan, that twisting, fleeing, piercing serpent. He is found guilty of carrying out the witchcraft curse, and he is being judged in the court of heaven right now. I break the curse now because it is illegal. Jesus already became a curse for me. Now I issue a restraining order against Leviathan in the name of Jesus. Amen.

If you feel led to do so, continue to pray in tongues. If you still have a headache or a swirling sensation in your breast or any other part of your body, keep praying through the decrees and prayers in this chapter until it breaks off you.

CHAPTER 7

TRAUMA, LEVIATHAN, AND WITCHCRAFT

By His breath the heavens are garnished; His
hand pierced the [swiftly] fleeing serpent.
—JOB 26:13

TRAUMA IS A part of life here on this earth. How we react to the traumas we experience makes a huge difference in the strength and permeability of the hedge of protection God has placed around each of us. If we allow bitterness to gain a foothold, that bitterness enables Leviathan to legally attack us. The story of Job, a biblical example of someone who endured severe trauma, illuminates the principles for us.

In Job chapter 1 we see how his life was engulfed by waves of severe trauma that originated from Satan, that old serpent who came into the presence of the Lord with the sole purpose to accuse Job. Here Satan said of Job:

117

Have You not put a hedge about him and his house and
all that he has, on every side? You have conferred prosperity and happiness upon him in the work of his hands,
and his possessions have increased in the land. But put
forth Your hand now and touch all that he has, and he
will curse You to Your face.

—JOB 1:10–11

The Lord was so confident of Job's integrity that He put all Job
had into Satan's hands, giving the enemy permission to test his
theory. This is what took place next:

There came a messenger to Job and said, The oxen were
plowing and the donkeys feeding beside them, and the
Sabeans swooped down upon them and took away [the ani-
mals]. Indeed, they have slain the servants with the edge of
the sword, and I alone have escaped to tell you. While he
was yet speaking, there came also another and said, The
fire of God (lightning) has fallen from the heavens and has
burned up the sheep and the servants and consumed them,
and I alone have escaped to tell you.

While he was yet speaking, there came also another
and said, The Chaldeans divided into three bands and
made a raid upon the camels and have taken them away,
yes, and have slain the servants with the edge of the
sword, and I alone have escaped to tell you. While he
was yet speaking, there came also another and said, Your
sons and your daughters were eating and drinking wine
in their eldest brother's house, and behold, there came a
great [whirlwind] from the desert, and smote the four cor-
ners of the house, and it fell upon the young people and
they are dead, and I alone have escaped to tell you.

—JOB 1:14–19

That is a massive amount of trauma. First Job experienced the
loss of all his oxen, donkeys, and even servants to enemy attacks.
Another wave of financial assault swooped in with further loss as

fire burned up his sheep and remaining servants. Then Satan mas-
terminded the biggest blow yet: he murdered all Job's children as
they gathered to celebrate the eldest son's birthday (v. 13). If that
weren't enough, Satan later struck the man himself, covering Job's
body with "loathsome and painful sores" from the top of his head
to the soles of his feet (2:7).

Job unquestionably experienced severe emotional and psycho-
logical trauma as a result of these harrowing events, which clearly
wounded his soul. He explicitly expressed his anguish throughout
the rest of the Book of Job, saying that his soul was bitter, mourning,
"vexed," and being "poured out" (7:11; 16:15; 27:2; 30:16). Each
time he referenced the state of his soul, it was intricately tied to the
traumatic experiences he endured.

It is essential to remember that these events were orchestrated by
Satan, who incited the Sabeans and Chaldeans to attack Job. It was
Satan who created a whirlwind from the desert to take out his kids.
And Satan was also able to generate sickness in Job's body.

What does this prove? That old serpent can manipulate people
into attacking you, create storms in the natural world to use against
you, and put sickness on your body. This is a crucial point to grasp
because it underscores the fact that the enemy has the power to
create traumatic situations to deliberately take you out.

To what end? Of course, he comes to steal, kill, and destroy
(John 10:10). But another of his main strategies is to wound you
through massive trauma so he can then create an opening in your
hedge to slither through. Remember, Satan acknowledged that
God had "put a hedge" around Job and everything he had, "on
every side." He then challenged, "But put forth Your hand now
and touch all that he has, and he will curse You to Your face"
(Job 1:10–11).

Again, Ecclesiastes 10:8 (KJV) says that if you break a hole in the
hedge of protection with which God has surrounded you, then a
serpent can come in and bite. Satan is very aware of this biblical
precept, so he tries to create massive amounts of trauma in your

life to ultimately wound your soul. Once this happens, he can use those wounds as a hole in the hedge to come in and attack you.

Marked on the Calendar

I want to pull another piece of insight from Job's story: Satan loves to mark special calendar celebrations in your life with devastating trauma. Look at how this took place in the life of Job's family:

> And there was a day when [Job's] sons and his daughters were eating and drinking wine in their eldest brother's house [on his birthday]....And behold, there came a great [whirlwind] from the desert, and smote the four corners of the house, and it fell upon the young people and they are dead.
>
> — Job 1:13, 19

Notice, Satan killed all Job's children—at once—on a very special day: *his eldest son's birthday*! Satan did this purposely. He loves to mark specific days with trauma so he can gain a foothold in your soul *for the rest of your life*! From then on he won't even have to work to get you wounded, because that marker will be there, tormenting you every single time it comes up on the calendar again, year after year.

Think about it: Did someone dear to you die on your or the loved one's birthday? Is the Christmas season difficult for you because a loved one passed at that time, even though you all violently fought for the person's recovery? Did a horrific crisis happen on a certain day, marking it in your memory for the rest of your life? Has that date since created deep grief and sorrow every time it comes up on the calendar? If so, Satan has accomplished his objective.

MATTER HOLDS MEMORY

Even more concerning is that any extreme shock, trauma, or grief that befalls you can be so intense that it actually etches and stores that trauma in the cells of your physical body.[1]

Science has proven that matter holds memory. Consequently, your body, which is made of physical matter, stores any trauma you go through in the cells that make up your bones, organs, and every part of your physical structure. When this transpires, it causes your body to experience a violent reaction when the memory or even the date of the trauma pops up again. People frequently report to me that years after an initial trauma, they have experienced a heart attack or something of equal severity on that particular calendar date or close to it.[2]

SATAN IS LOOKING FOR OPPORTUNITIES TO TRAUMATIZE YOU

Look at this interchange between God and Satan:

> The Lord said to Satan, From where did you come? Then Satan {the adversary and the accuser} answered the Lord, From going to and fro on the earth and from walking up and down on it.
>
> —JOB 1:7

This indicates that Satan is roaming the earth looking for not just someone to accuse but also someone to traumatize! And his tactic of wounding you through trauma really pays off. Consider what happened to Job, a man whom God Himself called "blameless and upright" (v. 8). He had a complete meltdown!

THE PATTERN

Throughout the entirety of chapter 3, Job vented concerning the pain in his soul that came from the colossal trauma he'd just experienced in chapters 1 and 2. The following verse in chapter 3 proves that his soul was wounded from all he faced:

> Why is light [of life] given to him who is in misery, and
> life to the bitter in soul?
>
> —JOB 3:20

Notice that Job says he is "bitter in soul." Many times when we are forced to walk through extreme amounts of trauma, we have the propensity to get bitter about it. This is part of what I call "The Pattern." It goes like this:

- Satan creates storms to traumatize you.

- You become so wounded by the trauma of the battle that you grow bitter about it.

- Out of that bitterness you curse yourself and other people.

- Then you wish you were never born and say that you want to quit or even die to go to be with the Lord.

Have you fallen into this pattern during times of high crisis? If so, you have come into agreement with Satan's plan to take you out. He is quite aware that the only thing that can allow him access to you is a hole that is broken into your protective hedge. Trauma creates the hole!

Note: if there are no breaks in the hedge, then you will walk in prosperity beyond what you can ever imagine. Even Satan has acknowledged this. Again, look at his own words:

> Have You not put a hedge about him and his house and
> all that he has, on every side? You have conferred pros-
> perity and happiness upon him in the work of his hands,
> and his possessions have increased in the land.
>
> —JOB 1:10

Get ready to experience healing and prosperity as the holes in your protective hedge are plugged up!

Job Releases Curses on Himself

Job became so wounded that he got bitter about it. In fact he began to curse himself, even confessing that he wished he were never born and could just go ahead and die!

Let's skim through chapter 3 so you can see how Job fell into The Pattern.

> After this, Job opened his mouth and cursed his day (birthday). And Job said, Let the day perish wherein I was born, and the night which announced, There is a man-child conceived....Why was I not stillborn? Why did I not give up the ghost when my mother bore me?...Or [why] was I not a miscarriage, hidden and put away, as infants who never saw light?...Why is light [of life] given to him who is in misery, and life to the bitter in soul, who long and wait for death, but it comes not, and dig for it more than for hidden treasures, who rejoice exceedingly and are elated when they find the grave?
>
> —Job 3:1–3, 11, 16, 20–22

Satan's plan to put Job into this pattern functioned like clockwork. The amount of trauma he placed on Job's shoulders crushed him under the weight. It caused him to become so wounded that he grew bitter, cursed himself, and even wished he were dead.

If you allow yourself to fall into this pattern because of trauma, you may find yourself becoming bitter, just like Job did. Then you might start uttering curses on yourself, such as "I don't want to live. I wish I had never been born. I wish I'd never seen the light of day." These self-inflicted curses are born out of your bitterness. You might even start agreeing with thoughts of death, saying, "I wish I could just die and go be with Jesus," essentially cursing yourself with your own words.

I want to give Job some credit here. Satan said to the Lord, "Put forth Your hand now and touch all that he has, and he will curse You to Your face" (Job 1:11). The devil was counting on the trauma making Job curse and abandon his God. Fortunately, even after all the crises, Job stood strong and "sinned not nor charged God foolishly" (v. 22).

TRAUMA, WITCHCRAFT, AND SERPENTS

However, although he did not curse the Lord, Job did something *almost* as destructive. He cursed himself! And as you will now see, that allowed witchcraft and the serpent Leviathan to come in and attack him even more.

Look at this revealing statement Job uttered in the middle of his bitter diatribe to curse himself and his birthday: "*Let those curse it who curse the day, who are skilled in rousing up Leviathan*" (Job 3:8, emphasis added).

Because of his ancient wisdom Job understood this spiritual precept: witches not only put curses on people, but they are also very skilled in rousing up and controlling serpents, like the spirit of Leviathan. Remember, witches curse and then incite and stir up Leviathan (serpents) to carry out their curses. Again, Leviathan is the muscle behind their incantations.

When Job cursed himself, he knew that a spirit of witchcraft would ensure that the curse was released and that it would then also arouse Leviathan to enforce it.

Here is what is so crazy about this. A person would have to be totally insane to release a witch and a powerful serpent against himself. Who would do such a foolish thing? Only those who are extremely wounded by trauma and bitter about the things they have experienced would.

WITCHCRAFT AND BITTERNESS

A causeless curse cannot alight. There must be an opening, and many times that cause is trauma and bitterness. Bitterness is closely linked to witchcraft. Recall the story of Simon the sorcerer. Let's see how bitterness caused him to operate in a witchcraft spirit.

> There was a man named Simon, who had formerly practiced magic arts in the city to the utter amazement of the Samaritan nation, claiming that he himself was an extraordinary and distinguished person. They all paid earnest attention to him, from the least to the greatest, saying, This man is that exhibition of the power of God which is called great (intense). And they were attentive and made much of him, because for a long time he had amazed and bewildered and dazzled them with his skill in magic arts.
>
> —ACTS 8:9–11

As you can see, Simon had mad skills when it came to witchcraft. It's a strange story, because even though he was totally immersed in practicing the dark arts, the Bible says he believed when he saw the signs and wonders of the Lord (v. 13)! However, the Bible also states that when he witnessed the Holy Spirit being imparted to people "through the laying on of the apostles' hands, he brought money and offered it to them, saying, Grant me also this power and authority, in order that anyone on whom I place my hands may receive the Holy Spirit" (vv. 18–19).

Peter was incensed that Simon would offer money for God's free gift, and he commanded Simon to repent. Then Peter said something very revealing about the root cause of why Simon operated in that spirit of witchcraft:

> For I see that you are in the gall of bitterness and in a bond forged by iniquity [to fetter souls].
>
> —ACTS 8:23

Here, Peter gets to the heart of the matter. Simon was a sorcerer because of the bitterness that was in his heart. I've encountered many witches in my time, and most of them have experienced extreme trauma—and even molestation—in their childhoods, which caused them to become extremely bitter. Then the trauma and bitterness led them to come into agreement with a witchcraft spirit.

Though the Scripture doesn't elaborate on Simon's past, I wouldn't be surprised if this was the case in his life. We see proof of this in the fact that he believed in the Lord, even desiring the Holy Spirit. Nevertheless, bitterness caused his belief system to be all twisted up (similar to the twisted, fleeing serpent).

Look again at Peter's statement to him: "You are in the gall of bitterness and *in a bond forged by iniquity [to fetter souls]*" (v. 23, emphasis added). Bitterness forges a bond in your soul to witchcraft! In fact this is how witchcraft "fetters" your soul. The word *fetter* means "a chain or manacle used to restrain a prisoner."[3] Do you see that bitterness chains you to witchcraft? It causes you to be controlled, like a prisoner, by that spirit, which then curses you and allows Leviathan and other serpents to carry out the curse.

This explains why Job would be so foolish as to not only curse himself but also release both witchcraft and Leviathan to carry it out. He was so bitter from the trauma Satan put him through that his soul was fettered—chained to those spirits that were controlling him.

GOD LECTURES JOB ABOUT LEVIATHAN

If you've read the entire Book of Job, you know that all ended well. The Lord turned the captivity of Job around and restored his fortunes, giving Job twice as much as he had before (Job 42:10). In fact the Lord "blessed the latter days of Job more than his beginning," with fourteen thousand sheep, six thousand camels, one thousand yoke of oxen, and one thousand female donkeys. He also had seven more sons and three more daughters (vv. 12–13). Then "Job died, an old man and full of days" (v. 17).

All is well that ends well, as the saying goes. However, Job's journey to get to that point was epic. Part of his learning curve was an expensive lesson concerning Leviathan. After Job's reckless invitation for witchcraft to curse him and for Leviathan to carry it out, God gave Job a lecture that took up an entire chapter of the Bible about the immense power of the principality he had just so flippantly engaged. Let's look at God's reprimand and consider the lessons we also need to take from it.

The Lord began by detailing the might and power of this king of all the serpents:

> Can you draw out the leviathan (the crocodile) with a fishhook? Or press down his tongue with a cord? Can you put a rope into his nose? Or pierce his jaw through with a hook or a spike? Will he make many supplications to you [begging to be spared]? Will he speak soft words to you [to coax you to treat him kindly]? Will he make a covenant with you to take him for your servant forever? Will you play with [the crocodile] as with a bird? Or will you put him on a leash for your maidens?...Can you fill his skin with harpoons? Or his head with fishing spears?
> —Job 41:1–5, 7

Just so you understand the might of Leviathan, the answers to each question is *no*. God was informing Job of the reality of his recklessness to invite this beast to carry out a curse against him, because Leviathan was nothing to fool around with.

Then the Lord brought even more clarity to the foolishness of messing with Leviathan:

> Lay your hand upon him! Remember your battle with him; you will not do [such an ill-advised thing] again!... No one is so fierce [and foolhardy] that he dares to stir up [the crocodile].
> —Job 41:8, 10

Here God Himself was admonishing Job with extreme stern-
ness: "You took on a principality that was out of your league,
buddy!" Yet we do the same! We flippantly go after this serpent,
not understanding the might he possesses as a high-level principality. The Lord's warning here is clear: "Remember your battle
with him; {never} do [such an ill-advised thing] again!" (v. 10).

Nonetheless, uninformed Christians scream and shake their
fists at this devil, attempting to bind, rebuke, and cast him out in
Jesus' name. Yet Isaiah 27:1 clearly says it's the Lord's "sharp and
unrelenting, great, and strong sword {that} will visit and punish
Leviathan the swiftly fleeing serpent."

God takes out Leviathan with His sword; you don't take him
out with yours. It happens as a result of your filing a case against
him in the court of heaven. Let me prove it to you.

TAKING LEVIATHAN TO COURT

When people find themselves overwhelmed, they often act hastily,
without a clear understanding of the principles that Jesus Himself
has established for us. Let's return to Luke 10:19, where Jesus gave
us "authority to trample on serpents and scorpions, and over all the
power of the enemy" (NKJV).

Again, the word *authority* (Greek *exousia*) holds a profound
meaning: "the power of judicial decision."[4] You don't deal with
Leviathan by rebuking and binding; instead, you take him to
heaven's court, *all in the name of Jesus*. Many will argue that this
is error, that we have the right ourselves to bind and rebuke any
spirit. However, here Jesus Himself informs us of the proper legal
procedure to deal with huge principalities and evil spirits: take
them to court.

When you harmonize this verse with Job 41:8 (instructing you
to lay hands on Leviathan, remember the battle, and never do such
an ill-advised thing again), as well as Isaiah 27, which clearly states
that God will slay this beast with *His* sharp, unrelenting sword,

you see that by the testimony of two or three witnesses, this matter is established (Matt. 18:16).

To further lay a foundation for this point, let's delve into the word *exousia* a bit further. It refers to not only judicial authority but also governmental authority—"the power of rule or government."[5] There is little understanding within the body of Christ concerning the judicial and governmental authority in which Jesus enables us to operate because of His work at Calvary.

Once again, look at this powerful courtroom verse from Daniel 7:

> I kept looking until thrones were placed [for the assessors with the Judge], and the Ancient of Days [God, the eternal Father] took His seat....The Judge was seated [the court was in session] and the books were opened.
>
> —Daniel 7:9–10

Clearly this is a scene from a courtroom in heaven. In fact it refers to the most powerful courtroom in the heavenly judiciary system, the Ancient of Days Court.

As we read on in chapter 7, we see that the main reason the court convened that day was to legally decree Jesus as Messiah and King over all.

> I saw in the night visions, and behold, on the clouds of the heavens came One like a Son of man, and He came to the Ancient of Days and was presented before Him. And there was given Him [the Messiah] dominion and glory and kingdom, that all peoples, nations, and languages should serve Him. His dominion is an everlasting dominion which shall not pass away, and His kingdom is one which shall not be destroyed.
>
> —Daniel 7:13–14

Do you see the majesty of this moment? Jesus, the Son of Man, was summoned to the Ancient of Days Court to appear before His Father, the judge of all the earth. For what purpose? So it could be judicially decreed that He, the Messiah, had been given ultimate authority over every people, nation, and tongue. It is here, in this court, that Christ was legally bequeathed everlasting dominion, which would never pass away. This decree was legally backed by the authority of the highest court in the universe. Because this was executed in the court system, no one could take that power away from Jesus. Hence, when Christ hung on the cross, He sacrificed Himself to legally enact and enforce what had already been decided in heaven's court system.

Now Jesus imparts to us the exousia (judicial power) He sealed with His sacrifice. We now have the power of judicial decisions over every serpent and over all the power of the enemy, based on the judicial authority granted to Him in heaven and carried out on Golgotha.

We need to cease randomly binding and casting out demons because we saw Jesus doing it in Scripture. Rather, we must meditate on the complete work of Christ on the cross and how it is judicial at its very core! Then we must do as Jesus Himself instructed: take them to court in His authority.

At this, people may still argue that we have the right to bind every spirit. The truth is, we do. However, we must go higher in our jurisdiction and do so *from* our ascended position in the courts, exercising the governmental exousia authority Jesus has imparted to us.

LEVIATHAN IS A FUGITIVE FROM THE LAW

Once again, look at Luke 10:19: "Behold, I give you the authority to trample on serpents and scorpions, and over all the power of the enemy, and nothing shall by any means hurt you" (NKJV). As we've noted before, the word *hurt* here signifies "to be a criminal, to have violated the laws in some way."[6]

These serpents are criminals. They have violated the law by carrying out witchcraft curses against us. This is illegal because Jesus has already borne the curse for us on His cross. Where do you take a criminal who has broken the law? To court, of course.

This principle applies to Leviathan and the other malevolent entities as well.

Leviathan is indeed a criminal, and this is why we can rightfully take him to court. Isaiah 27:1 in the King James Version calls Leviathan "the piercing serpent." The word translated as "piercing" or "fleeing" here means "a fugitive," which is someone on the run.[7] This makes Leviathan a fugitive from the law. Why? Again, because he enforces curses against us, despite the fact that Jesus has already taken upon Himself the curse for us.

We are not to lay our hand on Leviathan through binding, rebuking, or casting him out. Rather, by faith we arise into the court where we are seated in heavenly realms with Christ (Eph. 2:6, NLT) and where we have rights as citizens of heaven. Then we present our case to the court through the authority (exousia) that Jesus gave us. When Leviathan enforces curses against us, he is essentially breaking the law, because Jesus Christ has already borne the curse for us. This is the argument we bring to court. When we confront Leviathan in that place, we approach him with legal facts and scriptural truths as our ammunition, rather than merely uttering random words, like "I cast you out; I rebuke you." No, we bring a charge against this criminal with the power of a judicial decree.

THE CONSEQUENCES OF BATTLING LEVIATHAN OUTSIDE OF JUDICIAL AUTHORITY

I've often asked attendees of my meetings how many of them have taken on Leviathan by rebuking, binding, or casting him out, only to experience severe attacks afterward. The response has been overwhelming, with hundreds, perhaps thousands, of people raising their hands and sharing their horrifying stories.

For instance, I recall an incident in which a man and his best friend had been praying together for over twenty years. Every Tuesday they would meet to intercede, which is truly admirable. At some point they decided to focus their prayers on confronting Leviathan for a month straight. They prayed in the Spirit and earnestly sought to address this issue. However, the outcome was tragic. The man shared that after this period of intercession, he suffered a stroke, and his prayer partner passed away.

The Bible says, "My people are destroyed for lack of knowledge" (Hos. 4:6). Though their hearts were pure, these men made the serious error of taking on a principality outside of the judicial authority Christ gave us. When I met that man, he was walking with a cane, a lingering symptom of the stroke. I had him repent for laying his hands on Leviathan; then, through my own judicial authority, I asked the heavenly court to remove Leviathan by legal decree, in Jesus' name. Then I ministered healing to his body, and he was completely restored.

I also spoke with a pastor and his wife who had gone after Leviathan in the past without fully understanding the consequences. Tragically, during that period, the pastor's wife experienced a miscarriage. I told them the miscarriage could have been linked to Leviathan, as evidenced in Job 3, when Job was cursing the day he was born and loosing Leviathan on that day. Here Job said:

> Let those curse it who curse the day, who are skilled in rousing up Leviathan....Why was I not stillborn? Why did I not give up the ghost when my mother bore me?... Or [why] was I not a miscarriage, hidden and put away, as infants who never saw light?
>
> —JOB 3:8, 11, 16

I share these stories not to frighten you but to encourage you to break any past agreements you may have made with Leviathan through trauma, bitterness, or even making war against him in an erroneous manner.

OPENING A CASE AGAINST LEVIATHAN

Do you have your Communion elements ready? We're going to engage in a powerful activation.

First spend a few minutes worshipping and praying in tongues. As you do, you will ascend into the courtroom of heaven. Declare these scriptures concerning the Ancient of Days Court as you go up:

> *I kept looking until thrones were placed [for the assessors with the Judge], and the Ancient of Days [God, the eternal Father] took His seat, Whose garment was white as snow and the hair of His head was like pure wool. His throne was like the fiery flame; its wheels were burning fire. {Snakes hate fire.} A stream of fire came forth from before Him; a thousand thousands ministered to Him and ten thousand times ten thousand rose up and stood before Him; the Judge was seated [the court was in session] and the books were opened. {And then the power of the beast was taken away.}*
>
> —DANIEL 7:9–10

Now as you stand before this fiery court, think about the relentless traumas that have occurred in your life, possibly orchestrated by the enemy to wound you. Have you, with your own will, allowed bitterness to take root as a result? Take a moment to ponder this.

Wherever you've allowed trauma and bitterness to fester in your soul due to past crises, get your Communion elements ready, and let's put an end to this cycle and pattern right now, in Jesus' name. Declare these words, speaking them aloud:

> *Lord Jesus, as I stand before the Father, the judge of all the earth, I decree that I'm addressing the trauma the enemy put on my life head-on. I know that as I worship, pray in tongues, soak in fire, and take Your Communion, I will be healed of every wound the enemy has brought on me through repeated tragedies. So I ask that the wheels of fire on the judge's bench would go back in time to every place in my life where I was wounded through trauma and burn up those memories. I decree streams of fire are emanating from the judge's bench in the Ancient of Days*

Court, consuming every painful memory and altar of trauma within me. I command all chaff, every briar and thorn, and the wicked internal foe to be incinerated at this moment.

I decree that every special event, celebration, or date that has been marked by trauma from the enemy would be redeemed and that I would never be triggered on those dates again. I decree that all memories stored in my body, bones, and muscles at a cellular level would be completely incinerated, in Jesus' name.

I also refuse to tolerate bitterness in my life any longer. I repent for allowing myself to get bitter from all the crises I have endured. I repent for how bitterness caused me to release curses on myself and others. I break my agreement with wanting to give in, wishing I'd never been born, and wanting to quit and even die and go be with Jesus. I break my agreement with The Pattern Satan put me in, and I declare that I will never fall into that pattern again, in Jesus' name. Amen.

Now get your Communion elements and pray these words:

Lord, as I partake of these sacraments, I testify to the highest authority in the universe and in this court—the authority and power of Christ's sacrifice. Through His sacrifice, He crushed the head of the serpent and made all my victories possible. As I partake of the body and blood of Christ, I do it in remembrance of this great victory! My partaking of His body and His blood in the presence of this court is my ultimate testimony of victory over all the enemy's strategies.

As I take in the bread of life, I decree life to my body and my soul, recompense into my finances, unity into my marriage, and increase into my business and all my endeavors. I decree Christ's body is bringing life into every place the enemy is afflicting me with traumatic memories, to heal me completely.

As I drink the cup of His blood, I decree my sins of bitterness are totally washed away and my soul is refreshed, nourished, and strengthened in every area that has been wounded by the storms the enemy created in my life. I decree the blood is being slathered on every gate, door, and opening in my soul that was created by traumatic events so every demonic spirit has to pass over and cannot afflict my temple. I decree the blood is sealing up the breaks in my soul from trauma that caused my hedge of protection to be broken into. In Jesus' name, amen.

Now partake of the elements; then pray in fiery tongues for a few minutes.

Now, Lord God, the judge of all the earth, as I proceed to bring my case before this court, I first acknowledge that I was out of order when I laid my hand on Leviathan. I remember that battle, and I promise never to engage in such a foolish act again. I repent for any of my actions that were out of order. From now on, I commit to operating in my judicial exousia authority, according to the instructions of Jesus. I thank You for breaking the curse that was placed on me through engaging in Leviathan. I decree that through the power of Your cross, that curse is broken off my life.

Now, Lord Jesus, I release the exousia authority, which gives me the judicial power to file a case against Leviathan. I decree that he is a fugitive from the law because he enforces the curse against me when You have already become the curse for me by hanging on the tree. So, in Your name I stand here with the legal authority You Yourself have granted to me, which empowers me to trample on serpents and scorpions and overcome all the power of

the enemy—which includes every witchcraft and idola-
trous spirit.

Now declare these words:

Now I also decree that I'm under grace, not the law. For
where my sin increased and abounded through my idol-
atry, grace super-increases all the more. I'm acquitted by
grace, and I've been made righteous in Christ.

Thus, any accusations brought against me by idola-
trous spirits, witches, serpents, or Leviathan in this court,
I declare to be null and void, expunged from the record
because they are covered by the cleansing power of the
blood of Jesus and burned by the streams of fiery judg-
ments coming out of the Ancient of Days judge's bench. I
overcome every enemy through the power of grace and by
the blood of the Lamb and the word of my testimony in
this court.

I now exercise my exousia authority by requesting a
holy judgment from this court to be released against all
idols, Leviathan, and every other witch and serpent that
has been attacking me. I demand their arrest and the
restraint of their activities in my life by the power of the
judicial decrees Jesus imparted to me. I release a righteous
judgment against all idols, Leviathan and all serpents,
and the spirits of witchcraft, witches, sorcerers, diviners,
medium spirits, and wizards, in Jesus' name. I petition
this court for a restraining order to be placed on them all
now, leading to their arrest. Because of Jesus' name and
my exousia authority, they must submit to the orders of
this court—now! Father, I thank You for Your righteous
judgment.

Lord, I now command every curse that has been placed
on me to be broken! My soul has now been healed, ren-
dering the causeless curse ineffective. Jesus bore all curses

on my behalf while hanging on the tree, rendering them now illegal and broken.

Finally, demand restitution, saying something like this:

I am opening a legal claim in this court against the enemy. I place a legal demand through this court to receive sevenfold restitution for what the enemy has stolen from me, as I have caught him in the act. I firmly assert this claim so that it may be fulfilled and made manifest in my life—bringing healing, financial restoration, restored relationships, improved education, flourishing businesses, and recovery in every aspect of my life, including my property and belongings. I demand the immediate repayment of sevenfold restitution from the enemy, in the name of Jesus. Thank You, Lord.

CHAPTER 8

PYTHON SQUEEZES
OUT YOUR GAINS

As we were on our way to the place of prayer, we were met by a
slave girl who was possessed by a spirit of divination [claiming
to foretell future events and to discover hidden knowledge],
and she brought her owners much gain by her fortunetelling.
—ACTS 16:16

THE SPIRIT OF python is a master of camouflage, skillfully
wrapping itself around its prey, often going unnoticed until
it begins to squeeze the life out of its victim, causing the
person to feel like giving up or even dying. Let's examine its tactics
and the ways in which it operates.

My initial encounter with the python spirit was a period of deep
confusion and distress. At the time, I had no awareness that I was
grappling with this serpent spirit. All I knew was that I felt an
overwhelming desire to give up. It seemed as though my involvement in ministry was draining the life out of me, to the point that

I contemplated just leaving it all behind. The pain was so excruciating, I even considered pursuing a simple path, like working at a fast-food restaurant.

This period was also marked by intense depression, an unusual emotional state for me, as I've always been quite resilient to emotional swings. I found myself frequently shedding tears, which was totally out of character for me. My husband humorously refers to me as a Viking because I typically don't cry and am by no means easily moved.

I felt so utterly overwhelmed, even having thoughts of not wanting to continue living. That is when I knew that some dark force was at play, as that thought had never been on my radar before.

These issues intensified, and no matter how fervently I prayed, fasted, or repented, my distress persisted. Strangely the voice I heard—which I had initially thought was God's—kept telling me to *do more*: additional fasting, prayer, and worship, as if I hadn't already been doing those things in abundance.

I want to emphasize that these practices are indeed powerful tools for achieving breakthroughs in the spiritual realm. Countless times I've experienced a significant move of God after persevering in them. However, this situation was different. It felt imbalanced, as though I were being punished by God for not doing enough. Yet the voice continued to push me into a cycle of striving, where I felt forced to keep doing more, disconnected from the flow of the Holy Spirit and a genuine relationship with God. (I later realized the python spirit was pushing me to perform the law of rituals so it could bewitch and put a spell on me like it did the Galatians, who tried to fulfill the law through works of their flesh.)

At that time I was in the early stages of receiving revelation on serpents, but I hadn't encountered the python spirit directly. Thus, I was still unaware of the extent of its influence. However, one night while studying these demonic entities, I received the revelation about how fire drove the serpent the apostle Paul was carrying out into the open.

Inspired, I decided to immerse myself in God's fiery presence that evening. I played Jesus Culture's song "Set a Fire" and began singing along fervently. Then, in the middle of that night, I received a vision of a large python slithering through my garage.

In dreams garages often symbolize ministries. Immediately the Lord revealed that the python was trying to get me to quit so that my ministry would fail. Then the Lord explained that He had extraordinary plans for Katie Souza Ministries, that it would be used to bring healing to hundreds of thousands, even millions of people. Since the python spirit has divination capabilities, it had seen into my future and discerned our potential and the promises of God on our lives. Consequently the serpent had coiled itself around me, applying pressure to sap my determination.

I was both relieved and angered by this revelation. I was grateful I had heard from the Lord. (Demonic serpents put scales over our eyes and ears so we can't hear from the Holy Spirit. They squeeze out our ability to discern. But the fire burns them off!) However, the fact that I had been unaware of its presence bothered me to no end. The encounter highlighted the importance of what I had learned through Paul's story: that every believer needs to immerse himself or herself in fiery worship on a regular basis.

THE PYTHON SPIRIT MIMICS GOD'S VOICE

Once I saw the python, I asked God to give me more understanding about what had happened to me. I want to break down that revelation for you now from Acts 16.

> As we were on our way to the place of prayer, we were met by a slave girl who was possessed by a spirit of divination [claiming to foretell future events and to discover hidden knowledge], and she brought her owners much gain by her fortunetelling. She kept following Paul and [the rest of] us, shouting loudly, These men are the servants of the Most High God! They announce to you the way of salvation! And she did this for many days. Then Paul, being sorely annoyed and worn out, turned and said to the spirit

within her, I charge you in the name of Jesus Christ to
come out of her! And it came out that very moment.

—ACTS 16:16–18

This woman possessed the demonic skill of divination, which
means "the practice of seeking knowledge of the future or the
unknown by supernatural means."[1] As we noted earlier, the word
divination here is the Greek word *pythōn*.[2] So, clearly a python
serpent was the source of her demonic anointing and her ability to
foresee future events.

It's no coincidence that this woman intercepted Paul and Silas
on their way to prayer. This serpent opposes any efforts to advance
in prayer and ministry, thus hindering us from successfully ushering the kingdom of heaven to earth. The passage in Acts 16 says
she "met" them (Greek *apantaō*), which can be used "in a military
sense of a hostile meeting."[3] Alerted to their presence in the spirit,
the serpent controlling this woman had come to war against Paul
and Silas as they walked out their kingdom assignment.

In fact it was the python spirit that was speaking to Paul through
her the entire time. Do not forget that the serpent speaks! It did so
in the original garden, conversing with Eve, enticing her to sin with
its persuasive words. Sadly, it hasn't stopped since.

The following quote from *Thayer's Greek-English Lexicon* connects to this important point: "Some interpreters think that the
young woman here mentioned was a ventriloquist."[4] Do you know
what a ventriloquist is? It's "a person who can speak or utter sounds
so that they seem to come from somewhere else, especially an enter-
tainer who makes their voice appear to come from a dummy of a
person or animal."[5] The python spirit has many skills. Divination
is one of them, but throwing its voice is another. It can speak not
only into your mind but also through other people, making you
think you are engaging a human being, not a slimy serpent, and
causing you to give credence to their words.

Notice what this woman proclaimed about Paul and his com-
panions: "These men are the servants of the Most High God! They

announce to you the way of salvation!" (v. 17). Isn't it interesting that the snake's words sounded so godly and holy, even though they were deceptive?

The python spirit can cunningly mimic the voice of God. Consequently, since this spirit operates in divination, it may prophesy things that are entirely contrary to God's plan for your life. You could end up marrying the wrong person, entering an abusive relationship, quitting your job, or even disbanding your ministry—all in contradiction to God's will—if you do not discern that the python spirit is speaking to you.

That's what happened to me when I encountered the python spirit. The voice I was hearing left me in so much despair and confusion that I wanted to quit the ministry—and life as I knew it.

Even Paul Didn't Get It at First

Pythons, like every serpent, are masters of camouflage, so it's very hard to know when they are deceiving you with their words and squeezing the life out of you. Believe it or not, this snake even fooled Paul—at first, that is.

The servant girl followed and mocked Paul and Silas "for many days." Finally, "Paul, *being sorely annoyed and worn out*, turned and said to the spirit within her, I charge you in the name of Jesus Christ to come out of her! And it came out that very moment" (Acts 16:18, emphasis added).

Did you see that? She kept shouting Godlike proclamations for several days, and still Paul didn't pick up the presence of the serpent. When I read this passage, I felt vindicated that I didn't catch on right away that a python was attacking me. Like me, Paul knew something was wrong—he just didn't know exactly what. The Bible says Paul was "sorely annoyed and worn out" before he finally cast out that snake! This indicates that this serpent will exhaust and irritate you to no end, for as long as it can.

Let me add here that the girl "*kept following Paul* and [the rest of] us, *shouting loudly*" (v. 17, emphasis added). This demon will keep hounding you! It is persistent, and it will shout its lies loudly in your mind, as well as through people and your circumstances, until you catch it and cast it out.

Let me emphasize this: If you're hearing things that you believe are from God but they leave you feeling grieved, exhausted, frustrated, and drained, then it's likely you are hearing from a different source. God's Word and His presence bring refreshment and strength. Genuine revelation from God will always energize you.

You need fire and discernment to overcome the python's tactics, but it's also essential to be accountable to trustworthy spiritual leadership and authority figures who walk in purity and the fire of God's presence. Seek leaders who can confirm whether the guidance you are receiving is from the Lord. If two or three people are telling you they don't think it is the Lord who is speaking, it's time to question the source of the voice you're hearing.

Once the fire exposed that serpent, I repented for coming into agreement with it. I judged it and took up that python by unwinding it off my body and mind, then casting it out, in Jesus' name. I clearly remember that moment. I literally was able to take in a huge, deep breath. Immediately I was no longer suffocated, and I felt totally different. My joy, purpose, and commitment to God's call and ministry returned in full force. It was a profound shift, which then enabled me to set others free from that same oppressive demon.

TESTIMONY

Let me share an incredible story with you. Right after my deliverance I had the opportunity to attend a meeting hosted by A. A. Allen's granddaughter Cheryl Bryan. A. A. Allen was an amazing man of God known for his powerful tent meetings, where incredible miracles and deliverances took place. His ministry touched the lives of thousands, characterized by astounding displays of God's power.

Cheryl Bryan is one powerful chick. The first time I ever encountered her was at an event in Coeur d'Alene, Idaho. I was struggling and needed deliverance. She was sitting in front of me, and even though we had just met, she didn't hesitate to spin around and dispatch that demon—right in the middle of worship!

Years later she invited me to speak at an event she was hosting in the Lake Tahoe area. I flew into the airport, and she graciously picked me up. When she pulled up to the curb, I saw a look of total annoyance on her face. As I rolled my suitcase to the car, she flung open the trunk, grabbed my suitcase and whipped it inside, and then firmly slammed the trunk lid.

I stood there a little shocked, then asked, "Is everything all right?"

She started fiercely shaking her head *no*. Once we were seated in the car, she said, "No, I'm not OK. I don't know what's happening to me. I feel so overwhelmed and oppressed, and I just want to quit!" She vehemently added, "And I'm not a quitter! I've always been a fighter and have never backed down from a demonic attack, but I've never dealt with anything like this before." She said she had done everything to combat it—prayed, fasted, you name it—but she couldn't shake the feeling.

Suddenly, as she spoke, I saw a clear, open-eyed vision. Wrapped around her was a bright-green python. It coiled around her entire body, extending all the way past the top of her head. As I stared at it, the serpent turned, locked eyes with me, then taunted me by sticking out its pink tongue.

Since it was only my third time meeting Cheryl in person, I didn't think blurting out "There's a snake wrapped around you!" was a good idea, especially with other people in the car. Instead, I went to my hotel room, unsure what to do next. The meeting was starting in less than thirty minutes. However, I knew that for the event to be successful, we needed to get rid of that snake immediately.

So, I called Cheryl and said, "I need to speak with you privately before the meeting."

She replied, "We're already here praying."

Despite the circumstances I knew I had to proceed, so I rushed to the events center. When I arrived, I hesitated because everyone in the meeting was present, and I didn't want to share this in front of the entire group. Yet when I sat down next to her, she straight-away asked what was on my mind. I swiftly mustered courage and said, "While we were in the car, I saw a large python wrapped around you, and I believe that's the cause of your distress."

She stared hard at me for just a second, then firmly responded, "Get it off!"

I reacted, "Right here? Now?"

She practically shouted her yes.

In the vision I had seen the python's head, which gave me a rush of faith to be able to take it off. My body lurched as I snapped my arm out to firmly grasp where I had seen the serpent's head. Then, unwinding it from her whole body, I threw it into the abyss while commanding it to burn and never return.

Cheryl instantly underwent a remarkable transformation. Her countenance changed, and she took a deep breath, as if inhaling the *ruach* breath of God Himself. Then without hesitation she jumped up, full of energy, grabbed the mic, and rushed to the front of the gathering. Filled with newfound drive and vitality, she boldly exclaimed, "All right, everybody! Stand up! We are going to get delivered because we are all covered with snakes!"

At her command women across the room, from the front to the back, began fiercely pulling snakes off themselves, flinging them into the fiery pit. It was mass corporate deliverance on steroids!

When you are set free from the control of the serpent, you can immediately become a catalyst for revival. Energized by her deliverance, Cheryl wasted no time to release freedom to everyone present. It was an awe-inspiring moment.

Just a note: If you find yourself saying, "I feel depressed. I'm anx-ious. I need medication," don't automatically turn to pills or psy-chiatrists. First, recognize that you might be dealing with a spirit that needs to be cast out. It may be coiled around you, suffocating you, and pushing you to the point of giving up.

ACTIVATION

Now let's engage in an activation. If you've been feeling oppressed, lifeless, suffocated, on the verge of giving up, and burdened by a relentless voice commanding you to do more without results, you may have a python spirit wrapped around you.

Take this time to soak in fire, burning up the chaff in your soul that's letting that spirit in. The fire will also drive it out of hiding so you can see it!

Partake of the Communion elements, and break your agreement with the demonic beast. Then cast it out in Jesus' name!

THE PYTHON SPIRIT IS SQUEEZING OUT YOUR GAINS

Years ago I received a phone call from a dear friend whom I consider my spiritual mother. She reached out to share a perplexing experience with me. She stated that while in a car with a business associate, she looked over at this person and saw a vivid image—a green python snake wrapped around them.

Not coincidentally this person's business was facing difficulties. It wasn't thriving; instead, it was mired in a negative balance sheet. After a moment of prayer my friend asked me what I thought the python represented and what it was doing. I responded cautiously, suggesting that I pray more about it before offering an answer. After ending the call, I immediately went before the Lord and heard the word *gains*. When I looked it up in Scripture, it led me to this verse concerning the python spirit:

> As we were on our way to the place of prayer, we were met by a slave girl who was possessed by a spirit of divination [claiming to foretell future events and to discover hidden knowledge], *and she brought her owners much gain by her fortunetelling.*
>
> —ACTS 16:16, EMPHASIS ADDED

This slave girl had brought substantial financial gains to her masters through her ability to foretell the future. Because the word translated as "divination" is *pythōn* in Greek, it indicates that this demonic serpent can produce financial prosperity through its fortune-telling skills.

Think about how many illegal gains wicked people can generate. How do they do it? According to this story, the python spirit is behind it, through its ability to foresee upcoming events. Anyone would succeed in business if they knew ahead of time what the market was going to do. Thankfully, we have the Holy Spirit, who can outdo a demonic snake anytime and can lead us in financial paths of righteousness and prosperity!

Now, think about this for a moment. If a python spirit can bring in illegal gains for the wicked, what do you think that spirit will do to Christians? Its assignment is to squeeze out the financial blessings of believers, because that's what pythons do—they squeeze the life out of you, and that includes your personal wealth and business opportunities.

The good news is that the Bible says "the wealth of the sinner is laid up for the just" (Prov. 13:22, KJV). It has been prophesied for decades now that there would be a huge wealth transfer from the world into the coffers of those who follow the Lord, but we haven't really seen that yet. Why? I believe part of the reason is that Christians are crawling with snakes, including these python spirits, which squeeze out our gains. When the body of Christ gets de-snakified, then we will finally see that prophetic word manifest.

SNAKES AND MONEY IDOLS

Did you know that people in the region where Paul and Silas were preaching visited a temple to receive prophecies from an oracle believed to be inhabited by the spirit of python? They would seek her counsel to know the outcome of wars, political actions, and other future events, likely for financial gain. People in large numbers would bring their offerings and sacrifices to the temple, all in hopes of benefiting from the divining power of the python serpent.

Money is one of humanity's biggest idols. As you continue to read this book, please be alert for the Holy Spirit to show you if you've turned money into an idol in any way. If so, this would allow the python spirit to come in and squeeze out your finances.

FACING THE PYTHON IN COURT

So, what's our course of action? Well, once again, fire is needed to drive the python off your finances, but we must also face this serpent in court and overcome him with our testimony.

After Paul cast this spirit out of the slave girl, a significant incident unfolded: "When her owners discovered that their hope of profit {their gains} was gone, they caught hold of Paul and Silas and dragged them before the authorities in the forum (the marketplace), [where trials are held]" (Acts 16:19).

The masters of the slave girl did not like that the hope of their illegal gains was gone, so they kicked back. Controlled by the same python that had been on their witch, they took Paul and Silas to the marketplace, the place "where trials are held."

Satan, referred to as "that old serpent" (Rev. 12:9, KJV; 20:2), is also known as the "accuser of our brethren" (12:10). He continually stands before God in the court of heaven, accusing us day and night. He's always searching for a legal right to attack us. This is why the owners of the woman with the spirit of divination dragged Paul and Silas to court, charging them with a crime.

Like it or not, the python spirit speaks! He accuses you incessantly, saying you've made money into an idol, you're not tithing enough, or you're a poor steward. He will go into the court and testify that you have a history of gambling in your family or you often engage in excessive shopping. He constantly brings up instances of past wrongs, such as when you robbed and cheated people years ago. He meticulously identifies any financial or monetary sins in your life or within your bloodline, then takes them into the marketplace, where trials are conducted, and lays out those accusations to establish a legal foothold against you that will enable him to squeeze out your prosperity.

The woman's owners brought Paul and Silas before the "magistrates" (Acts 16:20), which can be likened to court officials. They accused Paul and Silas of being unwelcome Jews who encouraged unlawful practices and of throwing the city into great confusion. In reality Paul and his companion were doing none of these things. Instead, though no one would admit it, they were being tried for casting out the slave owners' moneymaking machine.

Look what happened to Paul and Silas because these accusations were lodged in court:

> The crowd [also] joined in the attack upon them, and the rulers tore the clothes off of them and commanded that they be beaten with rods. And when they had struck them with many blows, they threw them into prison, charging the jailer to keep them safely.
>
> —ACTS 16:22–23

Remember that all these things happened in the "marketplace," which was the area in a city where merchandise was bought, sold, and exchanged—where commerce was conducted. It was the hub of business and finance for the public. Paul and Silas were stripped naked, beaten with rods, and imprisoned right in front of all the bustling businesses and amid all the financial transactions.

This is the python's strategy against believers: to strip them naked of all their assets in the marketplace for all eyes to see and to strike them down with so many financial losses that finally their businesses, churches, and ministries get taken down. Then its hope is to imprison believers in a place of poverty as their wealth gets squeezed out.

The Power of Judicial Decisions Over Python

The good news is that even if the python drags you to court, you will always defeat those charges because of Christ. You have the blood! You have grace! Paul and Silas escaped their imprisonment miraculously by just worshipping the Lord and His goodness—right in the belly of that basement stockade.

Nothing can overcome the power of the cross to absolve every accusation this serpent can levy against you. But you must go to court to face those claims because the Bible is clear: we overcome the enemy "by the blood of the Lamb and by the word of [our] testimony" (Rev. 12:11, NKJV). Your testimony to the blood of Jesus' cleansing you of all sins associated with money will crush the head of this serpent.

Freedom will take place as you continue to decree the blood and the free, unmerited grace of Jesus. As it does, you can confidently release your exousia authority to trample on this serpent and over all the enemy that might try to harm you. The juridical decision that Jesus has bequeathed to you empowers you to file unbeatable cases against the python spirit, forcing him not only to unwind from your ability to prosper but also to repay you for whatever he has stolen from you.

Once he slithers away, you will be exploded into a new level of influence in the marketplace. Doors of favor that were once welded shut by his scales will fling wide open, and you will see that start-up finally take off, that business venture begin to prosper, that opportunity you've been waiting for drop into your lap!

Business Opportunities

Be vigilant! If you start hearing a voice driving you toward an investment that could be morally questionable or downright sketchy, be aware that you might be *hearing the voice of a snake*, attempting to lead you into wrongdoing so it can gain a legal foothold and squeeze out your profits.

Avoid falling for those seemingly easy but shady deals that promise quick gains. If something appears suspicious, it's likely the serpent planting those thoughts in your mind. Snakes have a way of enticing you into making moral mistakes, which then allows them to accuse you of being a criminal in court, subsequently enabling them to drain your profits.

TESTIMONIES

After receiving this revelation about the python spirit squeezing out our gains, I decided to take action against any pythons that might be operating within our ministry. We were feeling stuck, struggling to grow, facing challenges with donations, and encountering roadblocks in various areas. I knew I couldn't allow this situation to persist any longer.

One morning a friend informed me about a powerful group intercession call led by Ed Silvoso, a renowned apostolic figure. This group was specifically praying against Leviathan and the python spirit. I immediately joined the call, and we engaged in fervent prayer and spiritual warfare. The atmosphere was charged with fiery intensity, and soon I encountered the Lord in the spirit by receiving a vision.

In it I saw a massive building that symbolized everything—churches, businesses, ministries, homes, and more. As I approached the building's side door, I noticed it was securely padlocked, rendering it inaccessible. But when I reached out and touched the lock, it miraculously opened and fell away. (That's the power of revelation—it unlocks doors that were once sealed shut.)

As the door swung open, I distinctly heard the voice of God. He loudly exclaimed, "Stand back!" Startled, I flung myself against the wall behind the door. Peering through the crack between the hinges, I witnessed a colossal python slithering down the hallway, toward the exit. While I watched it depart the building, the Lord declared, "Python has left the building" (reminiscent of the famous statement "Elvis has left the building").

Remarkably, shortly thereafter, our ministry received a generous $100,000 donation!

This experience served as undeniable proof to me that when you remove the python's influence from your business, ministry, church, outreach, online broadcasts, projects, or any other endeavor, you will witness your gains begin to flow. Also, once you eliminate this demonic presence from all your providers and contractors, whether they handle social media, accounting, fulfillment, product sourcing, or any other role, you'll see the tide turning in your favor too.

I vividly recall a visit to my good friend Dr. Francis Myles' church, where a python that had been squeezing out the church growth and financial prosperity was exposed. I'll share Dr. Myles' testimony here.

> In our church, we were grappling with certain financial challenges. When Katie arrived and began sharing her revelation about the soul serpents, it was truly eye-opening on multiple levels. From a pastoral perspective, I had noticed something was amiss in our church. About a month before Katie's visit, I had gathered our intercessors and shared my concerns. I told them, "Something doesn't feel right within these church walls. Every time I step into the pulpit, I feel like I'm suffocating, and it's a strange sensation that I don't experience anywhere else."
>
> Little did I know that Katie would soon visit our church and receive a vision from the Lord revealing a python spirit entwined around our church building. She had no knowledge of my previous month's meeting. When Katie identified the python spirit, the entire congregation began to follow her in circles around the building to unwind the python from the church.
>
> Let me tell you, the impact was profound. My preaching surged to a whole new level, and my energy levels soared. The sensation I had experienced before—that suffocating feeling—vanished completely. Conversations within the

church community started buzzing with reports of financial breakthroughs and increased tithing. It was nothing short of phenomenal.

Plus, just moments after we broke the python spirit's hold, I received a text message from my father in Africa. He had secured a piece of property for me at an unbelievably low cost—a beachside property in Africa. This was a monumental milestone for me, as I had never owned land in my home country before.[6]

—DR. FRANCIS MYLES

After that experience I visited a church with a stunning facility. It spanned thirty-six acres with impressive buildings, including school facilities, a cafeteria, and the main sanctuary. However, it was disheartening to see an auditorium capable of hosting thousands with only two hundred to three hundred attendees. Over the years their membership and giving totals had dwindled, and some members on the worship team held doubts about healing and deliverance.

I led a session at the church on a Saturday morning, and I knew I'd have to make a swift exit when the meeting was over and head straight to the airport. I pushed the session to its very limit, maximizing every moment until the last second before we needed to rush out. I had been teaching on the serpent all weekend, and as I bolted off the stage, the atmosphere was electric. The worship team was playing an intense fire song while the congregation echoed with cries of "Fire, fire, fire!"

Then I saw it. A colossal green python was coiled around the entire facility, with its head concealed within the layers of its wrapped body. I could tell it had been there a very long time. However, because of the amount of fire being released through worship, it was stirring and slowly starting to move. The teaching and the fiery atmosphere had caught its attention, prompting it to awaken from its slumber.

Remember, if you can't spot the head of a serpent, it signifies that it's still deeply entrenched in its hiding place, requiring more fire to drive it out.

I had almost stepped off the stage when I saw it. So, I turned around and ran to the pastor who was playing the keys. I discreetly informed him of what I had witnessed and told him we would discuss it further when I got home. Later we had a phone conversation, and I instructed him to engage in seven days of fervent worship, singing in tongues, and marching around the facility to unwind the python.

They followed through with unwavering humility and dedication. During the last day of their warfare campaign, an astonishing event unfolded. One member of the worship team, who held a significant role in the church, had previously been skeptical about miracles. However, during one of the worship sets, he suffered a heart attack. Fellow congregants rushed to his side, commanding the python to release its grip and invoking the power of Holy Ghost fire. Miraculously, he experienced a complete healing.

Moreover, the pastor had a profound personal encounter. His closest childhood friend, a lifelong companion since their early days, had tragically passed away a few years before. Well, that day the pastor received a vision in which he saw his friend descend onto the church stage from among the great cloud of witnesses. The pastor, caught up in an ecstatic state, found himself amid an extraordinary celestial gathering while his departed friend prophesied to him about forthcoming events concerning him and the church.

This overwhelming experience left the pastor unable to walk, necessitating that his friends to carry him home. There he reclined on his couch for an additional five to eight hours, enveloped in an ecstatic state. The supernatural realm had opened up to him once the python spirit was banished.

Following this remarkable incident, the church's attendance surged, with people seemingly appearing out of thin air. Consequently offerings and financial support multiplied due to the expanding congregation.

OPENING YOUR CASE AGAINST PYTHON

I'm going to do something unusual here. As we prepare to enter the court, I'd like you to pray about sowing a seed. I've witnessed time and again that sowing a seed comes directly against the python and adds massive force against it, causing it to unwind.

Seeds carry fire, and there are numerous scriptures—over fifty, in fact—in both the Old and New Testaments that emphasize the significance of offerings at the altar, which were met with divine fire.

Do you remember when Solomon presented a monumental offering in 2 Chronicles 7? (See verse 5.) He brought an abundance of cattle and sheep, surpassing any previous offerings in Israel's history, and fire descended from heaven to consume all of it (v. 1)! That's massive fire! The fire on your seed will not only drive the python off your money but also incinerate the wickedness within you.

When we bring our offerings to the altar, something significant occurs: fire. This fire has the power to expose and expel the serpents, wherever they may be lurking. Your offering has power!

In fact I'd like to share an example from my own life. Please understand that I'm not sharing this to boast, and I certainly don't intend to pressure you into any specific action beyond what the Holy Spirit guides you to do. However, I recently made a substantial offering, which consisted of my entire salary for a year. It was very frightening at first to take that big of a step, especially since my husband was no longer operating his trucking company.

Yet in the midst of that I also had a huge feeling of expectation. Well, that faith risk paid off. Since that time, my husband and I have brought in almost three times my yearly pay—and that in only the first three months of the year! I can't wait to add up the totals when the year comes to an end.

BRING YOUR OFFERING INTO THE COURTS

The Bible instructs us to bring an offering every time we step into the heavenly court. "For the LORD is great and greatly to be praised; He is to be feared above all gods. For all the gods of the peoples are idols, but the LORD made the heavens....*Give to the LORD the glory due His name; bring an offering, and come into His courts*" (Ps. 96:4–5, 8, NKJV, emphasis added).

It's crystal clear that we are to bring an offering into His courts. The people seeking messages from the python spirit brought so much treasure to the temple of this demon god that the city where it was housed became incredibly wealthy. The passage in Psalm 96 addresses the futility of false idols compared to our God. When we enter His courts, we should bring an offering, and it will defeat the idols in our lives—including that of money, which the python uses to gain the legal right to encircle us.

Now prepare your seed and Communion elements; then pray with me.

> *Lord, as I step into the Ancient of Days Court, I give the glory due Your name by bringing my offering with me in accordance with Psalm 96. I believe as I plant my seed in this court that I will receive a massive harvest—so big that I will not be able to contain it all!*
>
> *As I plant my seed, I decree the words of Daniel 7 that the judge is now seated, the court is in session, and the books are open. As I bring my case before this court, I decree that justice will be served and I will see the beasts slain and their power taken away.*
>
> *As this case commences, I humbly request that the books of my destiny be opened and read aloud, including everything recorded in them about my future successes, finances, businesses, ministry, church, savings, investments, and entrepreneurial and creative projects, including my web creations and social media platforms. May the books concerning my upcoming extravagant wealth be read out loud, then fulfilled by the angels present in this court, in the mighty name of Jesus.*

> *I also request that the books containing accusations made by the enemy against me in connection to my finances be opened so I can plead the precious blood of Jesus over these accusations.*

As we go through this process, let us actively repent and apply the cleansing power of the blood of Jesus to every accusation. Please join me in this prayer of repentance. Get ready to take Communion at the end of this prayer:

> *Father, I now humbly repent for any involvement in gambling, cheating, robbery, or greed. I place these actions and behaviors under the cleansing blood of Jesus. I ask for forgiveness for any past actions that were motivated by greed or that caused harm to others. Lord, I repent for any instances of cheating or taking advantage of people, for prioritizing personal gain over fairness and integrity. I repent for any financial mismanagement and wastefulness: for making unnecessary purchases, setting up unused monthly subscriptions, or spreading Your resources too thin. I repent for any misappropriation of funds or any dishonest scales in the marketplace. I repent for times when I have overspent, engaged in excessive shopping, or misused money. Lord, I also repent for any involvement in shoplifting, theft, embezzlement, or bad stewardship. It's time for me to reflect and repent. Being a good steward of Your money is essential. I repent for withholding my tithes and spending it instead on my idols.*
>
> *Father, cleanse me and make me pure and holy through the blood of Your Son, Jesus, right now. If I have ever gained illegally through the serpent, I renounce any agreement with the serpent in the name of Jesus. Jesus, let Your blood cover me completely—not only for my own sins but also for the sins of my ancestors and my parents, if they were involved in any of these actions. I decree through the*

power of Your Spirit that I will walk in righteousness in my finances from this moment on. In Jesus' name, amen.

Hold up the Communion elements and say:

Now as I take Communion, I decree that the life-giving power of Your body will bring life to my savings, investments, businesses, ministries, endeavors, and every part of my finances. I also decree that because of Your blood, every handwritten regulation or accusation that stands against me concerning my finances has already been nailed to the cross because I am the righteousness of God in Christ. I'm a new creation, and I stand firmly under Your grace.

Now partake of the elements; then make the following decrees:

Now, I stand in the Ancient of Days Court, commanding the streams of fire coming forth from the judge's bench to drive the serpent out of hiding and burn it to a crisp. I decree these flaming streams of fire emanating from the judge's bench are releasing fiery judgments against the enemy now.

Lord God, I also declare that the wheels of fire adorning the judge's bench will travel back through time to consume every altar dedicated to the python spirit and to financial greed, extortion, robbery, and cheating.

In addition, Father, I beseech You to purge from my soul anything that obstructs my financial gains, in Jesus' name. Thus, I decree the fire in this court is not only burning up the serpent, driving it from its hiding place, but also consuming the chaff within my soul that is sabotaging my finances and success.

I receive the ministry of the fiery wheels on the judge's bench to go back in time to every place and cause in my soul that caused me to have something in common with Python and that allowed that spirit to have an opening in the hedge of protection around my finances. As God's holy fire burns up the chaff in me, I also decree that the fortune-telling, divination spirit that is in charge of illegal gains is burning up right now. I judge that demon spirit of witchcraft by my exousia authority to release the power of a judicial decision against it, in Jesus' name. (Pray in fiery tongues.)

Note: As I write this, I'm seeing a vision of God wearing spectacles, meticulously searching and seeking out every hidden corner where the python spirit has nestled and wrapped itself around anything or anyone connected to your ministry, business, church, investments, savings, and advisers.

Now we are going to intercede for the sins of all those with whom we work, including those handling our finances, making investment decisions, serving as accountants, or managing our social media platforms. We repent on their behalf because the serpent may be hindering our gains by influencing them.

Father, I now intercede against the sins of every person, company, contractor, wholesaler, or business with whom we are connected in our pursuit of increasing gains for the kingdom. Father, we repent for their sins related to money, and we apply the blood of Jesus over them. (Remember that we have the legal right to ask God to forgive others' sins, as Jesus told His disciples after His resurrection [John 20:23]). *Therefore, Father, we intercede and forgive the sins of everyone we're working with who is connected to our finances. We do this so they can be free of the accusations brought by the python spirit in the marketplace, which are squeezing out our gains.*

Now play some fiery worship music as you take your wallet, purse, checkbook, or phone and prophetically unwind the serpent from your finances. Decree that you are releasing your exousia authority against him and that by judicial decree he has to unwind off your finances.

Prophetically take up these serpents and unwind them from your mortgage, credit cards, debts, car payments, savings and checking accounts, investment and brokerage accounts, school loans, and any other financial responsibilities in your life. Then cast those beasts into the fire and command them to burn and never return.

Make these decrees:

> *Now I commission financial angels to go forth. As it's written in Deuteronomy 8:18, You, Lord, give us power to create wealth. The word* power *signifies not only the strength of God but also the strength of His angels. I release these angels who empower us to create wealth. May they align us with open doors, grant us revelations, and lead us to opportunities that bring financial blessings into our lives right now, in the name of Jesus. Amen.*

As you experience breakthrough in this area of your life, please pray about giving to our worldwide prison outreach, Expected End Ministries. You can learn more about our work at katiesouza.com /prison-outreach.

CHAPTER 9

HEALING AND DELIVERANCE FROM IDOLS

{They} served their idols, which were a snare to them. Yes,
they sacrificed their sons and their daughters to demons.
—PSALM 106:36–37

I N THIS CHAPTER and the next we will be pursuing deliverance
and healing from the demonic three-cord strand of idols, witchcraft, and serpents. Have servings of Communion ready.

The Bible states that when the Israelites worshipped idols, they
were placing their lives in the hands of evil spirits. Thus, if you
turn anything into an idol—whether it be money, family, possessions, social media, or even food—it will invite a demonic power
to assault you. In fact idolatry causes a snowball effect, allowing
an open door for a witchcraft curse to then land on you, with a
serpent accompanying to carry it out. Again, I offer proof:

> Cursed is the man who makes an idol or a molten image,
> an abomination to the Lord, the work of the hands of the
> craftsman, and sets it up in secret.
> —DEUTERONOMY 27:15, NASB

Idolatry is a sin that breaks a hole in your hedge of protection; then that sneaky snake comes in to bite you.

IDOLS ARE DEAF, DUMB, BLIND, AND LAME

This demonic three-cord strand often leads to a wide variety of sicknesses and diseases.

Did you know that the Bible says idols are deaf, dumb, blind, and lame? For example, Psalm 135:16–17 says, "[Idols] have mouths, but they speak not; eyes have they, but they see not. They have ears, but they hear not." And the Book of Revelation tells us that the people "did not stop worshiping demons, and idols of gold, silver, bronze, stone and wood—idols that cannot see or hear or walk" (9:20, NIV).

What does this indicate? First of all, since idols can't see, hear, or speak, their presence in your life can make it extremely difficult for you to see in the spirit, hear the voice of God, and speak an accurate prophetic word. Consequently they hamper the operation of your gifts. I will not go into depth about this now, but you can get the total download in the book *Idols Riot!*, written by me and my good friend Dr. Francis Myles.

To summarize, when you have turned anything into an idol, you can also have these kinds of issues manifest in your physical body.

BIBLICAL EXAMPLES

Let's start with a deaf and dumb spirit that is connected to idolatry. Again, the Bible says idols "have mouths, but they speak not" and "have ears, but they hear not" (Ps. 135:16–17).

A deaf spirit can encompass issues that include not only total deafness but also hearing loss; tinnitus; ringing, buzzing, and roaring in the ear; ear infections; and more. A dumb spirit can cause muttering and stuttering in speech and even make a person totally mute.

I remember the first time I saw a demon spirit that caused people to have speech problems and be mute. It had scaly, reptilian skin grown over its mouth so it could not speak. Notice how this demonstrates the agreement between idols and scaly serpents.

Let's look at a powerful illustration of someone in the Bible who was deaf and dumb because of possible idolatry in the family's life. It is demonstrated in Mark 9:17–27 and Matthew 17:14–18. When we harmonize these two Gospels, you'll see that in this story the poor boy's deafness and dumbness may have been caused by idolatry in his bloodline.

First, Mark 9 says this:

> One of the throng replied to Him, Teacher, I brought my son to You, for he has a dumb spirit. And wherever it lays hold of him [so as to make him its own], it dashes him down and convulses him, and he foams [at the mouth] and grinds his teeth, and he [falls into a motionless stupor and] is wasting away. And I asked Your disciples to drive it out, and they were not able [to do it]....And [Jesus] asked his father, How long has he had this? And he answered, From the time he was a little boy. And it has often thrown him both into fire and into water, intending to kill him. But if You can do anything, do have pity on us and help us....But when Jesus noticed that a crowd [of people] came running together, He rebuked the unclean spirit, saying to it, You dumb and deaf spirit, I charge you to come out of him and never go into him again.
> —MARK 9:17–18, 21–22, 25

This evil demon had been torturing the boy his whole life and often tried to kill him. Jesus identified it as a "dumb and deaf" spirit, then quickly dispatched it. *Thayer's Greek-English Lexicon* says the word translated "dumb" (Greek *alalos*) means "speechless, dumb, lacking the faculty of speech...*because the defects of demo-niacs were thought to proceed from the nature and peculiarities of the demons by which they were possessed*" (emphasis added).[1] This definition makes clear that the nature and particularities of this demon, which was deaf and dumb itself, were causing the boy to display the same characteristics.

I believe the deaf and dumb spirit on that child was connected to an ancient idol in his family's daily life or bloodline. According to Matthew 17:15, this child was epileptic, or "moonstruck." The moon goddess was one of the most commonly worshipped idols in ancient times. Even today many deify the moon, and its cycles are used to help witches, warlocks, and sorcerers cast evil spells on people to gain more authority over their lives. This further proves the connection between idols and witchcraft.

TESTIMONY

I went swimming late one night to unwind after a very long day in the studio. As I floated in the water, I looked up and noticed there was a full moon. Though it was stunning in appearance, I wondered what malevolent force was using its God-given majesty to release curses on people.

The next day some contractors were working at my house. The Holy Spirit pointed out a man to me, telling me to pray for him. When I did, he shared that the evening before (during the full moon), he had suffered a violent epileptic seizure. Immediately, I knew he was "moonstruck"; thus, there was idolatry and witchcraft somewhere in his life.

So, first I prayed trauma off of him and released major flames of fire to burn up the chaff in his soul and drive the serpent out of hiding. (A few years back he had suffered a horrible car crash while driving to his grandfather's funeral. Double trauma.) Then I had him renounce all idolatry, witchcraft, and serpents while I covered him in the blood and grace of Jesus. Next I broke the witchcraft curse that was on his mind, judged that idolatrous moon spirit, and then cast them all out, along with every serpent, by order of the court of heaven, in Jesus' name. I finished with a command for his brain to regenerate in every place it had been damaged.

There was so much power present that this man almost fell out; he leaned forward hard into my hand, which was wedged against his forehead. When I was done praying for him, he immediately looked different. He said he was experiencing tingling in his whole body, his mind was clear, and he felt something lift off his back. The Lord broke the curse and took that moon goddess and snake off his life.

THE DEAF ADDER

So, is there a connection between snakes and deaf ears? Recall the encounter I experienced when God revealed to me that I had religious tendencies that needed repentance. Bottom line, I thought my cutting-edge revelations were better than others'. Well, that religious pride and the idolizing of my philosophies had a snake on it; it was called the "deaf adder that stops the ear." (See Psalm 58:4.) When I got rid of it, my left ear popped open. (See chapter 1.) That deafened serpent works closely with deaf, idolatrous spirits to bring about hearing issues of all sorts.

TESTIMONIES

Here are just a few testimonies from people who took up serpents by pulling them out of their ears in my meetings.

I recall a young woman in her early thirties who had been deaf in her left ear since her teenage years. She did the activation and said she saw a vision of snakes coming out of her ear. Instantly, her ear opened, and she could hear for the first time since she had been a teenager.

Another woman told me she felt vibrations in her right ear when she pulled the snake out of her ears, and she started singing. She said she had never experienced anything like that so it was a bit uncomfortable. I responded by telling her she would be able to hear the Lord more clearly than before because now the vibrations and frequencies of God could flow through her. I spoke with her later, and she confirmed both to be true: her ears had opened in the natural, and she was receiving divine insights.

This woman said she'd had problems with her ears her entire life, with constant itching and pain. But after removing the serpents, her right ear didn't itch anymore.

I also remember a man in one of my meetings who had a deaf ear. He removed a serpent from his ear after admitting to being religious-spirited, and instantly his ear opened up.

ACTIVATION

So, let's pray in the Spirit and ascend into the grace court.

Decree aloud Hebrews 4:16: "Let us then approach God's throne of grace with confidence, so that we may receive mercy and find grace to help us in our time of need" (NIV).

Now present your testimony and get ready to take Communion.

> Lord God, I step boldly into this court of grace to receive grace and mercy in my time of need. Mercy triumphs over judgment, and grace supersedes the law, so I know in this court I will always be found innocent because of the blood of Jesus and grace.
>
> I humble myself before this court first through my repentance, knowing that God gives grace to the humble. Thus, I begin my testimony by repenting of the idolatry that has allowed the deaf and dumb spirit to come upon me. (Take time to confess any specific idols you have created in your life.)
>
> Now, Lord, as I take Communion, I do so in remembrance of You and Your victory on the cross, where You died to cleanse me of all my sins. I decree that as I drink this cup of Your blood and eat Your body, my sins are

forgiven. A "not guilty" verdict from this court concerning breaking the first commandment will be enforced and sealed by the power and testimony of Your body and blood, in Your name. Also, as I drink the cup of Your blood, I decree that my soul is nourished, refreshed, and strengthened. Thus, as I eat Your flesh and drink Your blood, my soul will never hunger or thirst for idols again.

I also decree that as I partake of Your supper, in remembrance of what You accomplished on the cross, the serpent's head is being crushed now, in Your name! Thus, no deaf adder can stop my ear, no deaf spirit can block my ears, and no mute spirit can put its scales over my mouth to cause me to be mute.

Every spirit must let go of me because Jesus took the handwritten requirements that were hostile to me and nailed them to the cross! I also decree to every demonic spirit afflicting me that Jesus has made a public spectacle of you through the cross. As I partake of Your body and Your blood, I celebrate and commemorate that moment. In Jesus' name, amen.

Now partake of the elements.

Now, as I stand in this grace court, I decree free, unmerited grace over my life. Although I cannot keep the whole law because of the weakness of my flesh, Jesus fulfilled the righteous requirements of the law on my behalf! He has done something I could never do. I announce this truth to every spirit that has been attacking me! I receive grace and mercy from this court to supersede my sins and idolatry. Because of grace I am acquitted of all the enemy's charges, and I am justified and in right standing with God.

Now pray in fiery tongues, or sing along to a song with "fiery" lyrics. Then declare this:

I decree right now that the fire of God is burning up the chaff in my soul, burning up the idols, and driving the serpent out from my ears into the open.

I also release my exousia authority against the deaf and dumb spirit, the witchcraft spirit, and every serpent, in Jesus' name. I decree that every evil altar of idolatry in my bloodline going back three generations is judged. They must break apart, pour out their ashes, and become ineffective in my life (1 Kings 13). Through the name of Jesus and the power of the heavenly judicial decrees, I command the witchcraft curse to be broken and the idolatrous spirits and serpents that are responsible for any deafness, ringing, buzzing, pain, infections, and itching in my ears to come out!

Put your fingers in your ears, and speak this command out loud:

Now, in the name of Jesus, I break every curse and command you, deaf and dumb spirit, to come out, and I command my ears to open—now! I command infections to die and any ringing and roaring in my ears to stop. Tinnitus, cease, in Jesus' name.

Pull that "deaf adder that stops the ear" out of your body, and command your ears to open, in Jesus' name! Then continue by speaking these words:

Now I command a creative miracle to happen in my ears. Every ear apparatus, be re-created right now, in Jesus' name.

Pull the serpent out of your mouth and the scales off your lips, in Jesus' name, and command your vocal cords, mouth, tongue, and every speech apparatus to be fully re-created, in Jesus' name!

BLINDNESS FROM IDOLATRY AND THE SERPENT

Many times idols are also behind blindness and other vision issues. As a case in point consider the story of blind Bartimaeus in Mark 10:46–52. The Bible tells us that Bartimaeus sat in the streets of Jericho, begging for his existence because he was sightless—that is, until Jesus healed him.

As I read this story, the Holy Spirit pointed out something I had never seen before. The scriptures connected the blind man with his father, noting that the name Bartimaeus means "a *son of Timaeus*" (v. 46, emphasis added). I thought this was odd, as I had seen no other examples of people who were healed by Jesus being called by a parent's name. Because the Holy Spirit was highlighting this, I looked up the father's name.

The name Timaeus, according to *Thayer's Greek-English Lexicon*, comes from the word *ṭāmē'*, which means "unclean."[2] As we look deeper to the prime root of this word (its verb form), however, we find that it means "to be or become unclean sexually, religiously, ceremonially." It also means to "be defiled…by idolatry."[3]

This indicates that Timaeus had religiously and ceremonially defiled himself with idols so much that he had not only corrupted himself but also stained his own family with his sin! As the head of his household, he probably led them to worship the idols he venerated. Because the Scriptures say idols have "eyes, but cannot see" (Ps. 115:5), I believe Timaeus' idolatry caused his son Bartimaeus to become blind.

MIRACLE TESTIMONIES

As I share the following testimonies, remember that before his conversion the apostle Paul idolized his false religious belief system, and it caused serpent scales to cover his eyes. Any type of idolatry in someone's life or bloodline will invite a curse and then cause serpent scales to cover that person's eyes, blinding him or her in many different ways.

I want to share a story from my time at a women's conference in Baltimore, Maryland, where I encountered a lovely woman who was deeply devoted to the Lord. She had a peculiar issue—a cataract in her eye. Despite her strong faith something in her bloodline seemed to have allowed a serpentlike presence to afflict her. We gathered a group of women to pray for her, spending an hour on this task. Progress was made as the cataract significantly reduced in size, and her vision became somewhat clearer. However, the group couldn't completely eliminate the last remnants of the issue.

Finally, one of the ladies asked for my help, as they were at an impasse. The woman with the cataract then came to me, saying the remaining portion of it looked like a "scale." The moment she mentioned that word, I immediately recognized the issue was a serpent scale that needed to be judged in the court of heaven. So, I guided her to repeat after me, saying, "In the name of Jesus, I judge..." As soon as we uttered the words, she exclaimed, "Oh, there it goes! It's gone!" A simple judgment from the court had removed that serpent scale, bringing total healing.

I once met a woman who suffered from a medical condition characterized by chronic blurry eyesight. When she acted on Jesus' words about taking up serpents (that is, removing "what is attached to anything"[4]), she pulled a serpent out of her eye. She said her eyesight immediately became crystal clear. She had also been experiencing neck pain for forty years due to a food allergy. Remarkably, when the snake was removed, that pain also disappeared. I can't resist connecting that serpent to her neck pain and food allergy, as the serpent in the garden also used food to harm people from the beginning.

In another incredible case a woman said she was constantly dealing with water dripping from her eyes, an issue that persisted for years. She had even scheduled surgery to address it. However, during one of my sessions she repented of a religious spirit, and instantly the serpent came out. Her excessive tearing ceased, and she canceled her surgery.

ACTIVATION

Now let's judge that blind, idolatrous spirit, the serpents, and their scales. If you suffer from eye issues, stop and take Communion now, pray in fiery tongues, and worship the Lord until you get your total breakthrough.

> *Lord God, I break the curse that has been placed on my eyes! I judge those idolatrous, blind spirits and cast them out, as I pull the snakes out of my eyes now, in Jesus' name! I judge the scales that have been covering my eyes. I command them to fall off like they did for Paul, and I command my eyes and all my vision apparatuses to regenerate now, in Jesus' name!*

IDOLS CANNOT WALK

The Bible says humankind "did not stop worshiping demons, and...idols that cannot...walk" (Rev. 9:20, NIV). Idols can cause you to be crippled in your physical body and suffer from various diseases like rheumatoid arthritis, scoliosis, bone deterioration, disc degeneration, and a wide assortment of other skeletal and muscular issues.

These idolatrous spirits can also cause birth defects. A biblical example of this is found in Acts 14, where a man, lame from birth, received a jaw-dropping miracle. Look at the Bible's description of how this amazing story unfolded.

> Now at Lystra a man sat who found it impossible to use his feet, for he was a cripple from birth and had never walked. He was listening to Paul as he talked, and [Paul] gazing intently at him and observing that he had faith to be healed, shouted at him, saying, Stand erect on your feet! And he leaped up and walked.
>
> —ACTS 14:8–10

As this man listened to the apostle Paul's preaching, he received faith to be healed of the birth defect that had afflicted him for decades. At Paul's command, he leaped up and was perfectly whole!

The response from the surrounding crowd was shocking! Look at what they did.

> And the crowds, when they saw what Paul had done, lifted up their voices, shouting in the Lycaonian language, The gods have come down to us in human form! They called Barnabas Zeus, and they called Paul, because he led in the discourse, Hermes [god of speech]. And the priest of Zeus, whose [temple] was at the entrance of the town, brought bulls and garlands to the [city's] gates and wanted to join the people in offering sacrifice.
>
> —ACTS 14:11–13

Lystra was a city so dedicated to idol worship that the people thought Paul and Barnabas were the gods they venerated, come down to earth to perform this miracle. The citizens of Lystra, along with their priest, a worshipper of the demon god Zeus, wanted to offer sacrifices to Paul and Barnabas. Typically they performed these types of sacrifice to service their demon gods. No wonder that poor man had been born lame. Idolatry ran in his bloodline! Idols can't walk; they are lame. Thus, the people who worship them will display those same characteristics.

MIRACLE TESTIMONY

I'm going to share two testimonies that are connected to folks who were lame or suffered deformities from the womb, just like the man in Lystra.

I was in a meeting in Baltimore, sitting in the front row and getting ready to preach a message on serpents. As I joined in the worship, I thought the worship leader, whom I'll call Stacy, was bent down on her knees, because she was singing into a microphone that was much lower than everyone else's. However, when I later stepped up on the platform, I realized she was standing fully upright. Although her torso was the same length as mine, a deformity caused her to have very short legs.

The next day, while I was in the green room eating lunch, Stacy came in to also grab a bite to eat. That's when she told me about a dream she'd had two days before the conference.

In it she'd seen a kangaroo walking toward her from a field with a baby in its pouch. As she looked at it, she suddenly realized a python was wrapped around the kangaroo's whole body. As the kangaroo walked past her, she heard the phrase "broken bones."

Immediately I knew what the dream meant. I said to Stacy, "Kangaroos don't walk; they hop. Your mother is the kangaroo, and you are the baby in the pouch. While you were in the womb, the python was wrapped around you both, and it broke your bones—which is why you were born like this!"

Stacy gasped, then added that her mother had died of a respiratory disease. I responded by telling her the python had not only affected the development of her legs but also squeezed the breath out of her mom, killing her.

When I asked Stacy if she was ready to pray, she nodded vigorously. I put my hand on her head and said, "I go into the heavenly court and demand justice for you against that python spirit in Jesus' name! I go back in time to where that snake first came in, and I command it to unwind from Stacy now!"

That was all it took. Immediately Stacy started screaming, "Woahhhhh" as she shot up under my hand, saying she felt like she was launching off the floor! Other people in the room jumped in to prophesy over her, declaring she would grow even more while she was in the car driving home—which is exactly what happened.

Within a few hours Stacy had sent me two separate videos. In the first she was sitting in the driver's seat of her car with the seat pushed all the way forward, explaining that was the position it had needed to be in for her to reach the pedals. She pointed out that *now* because of the elongation of her legs, her knees and feet were bent so much that it was uncomfortable for her to drive that way.

She then proceeded to back the seat up three times before she felt she landed in a good spot, commenting that she felt she could go back even farther.

The second video came a couple of hours later, once Stacy stopped to get gas. When she got out of the car and started walking, she felt that the arches in her feet were raised up. She got back in the car, took her shoes off, and placed one foot on top of the steering wheel while her friend videotaped the testimony. The footage showed an arch in her foot that she explained hadn't been there before. She said her husband would later confirm this because he rubbed her feet all the time. She added that throughout the whole trip, her feet had been going numb and were itchy and that she'd had to push her seat back two more times!

I also had the privilege of praying for an inmate who had been born with a cleft palate, which caused him to have two metal rods put in his mouth during his childhood. I prayed for all his trauma to be healed; then I led him to renounce any idolatry, witchcraft, and serpents in his bloodline. Finally I addressed the point where the curse had come in the first place. I demanded justice be given to him as I cast those spirits out, and then I commanded the metal in his body to melt. Here is his testimony in his own words.

> My name is Marquez, and you see, I was born three months early, with a hole in the roof of my mouth. I underwent surgeries as I grew older, and I had two metal pins put in on one side. Those two pins were keeping me from expanding my mouth to open it more.
>
> Before I could only open my mouth to a certain point. I could only get it to open so far, but during the service, Miss Katie…was actually looking for somebody else to pray for. I was trying to tell her where he was—because I knew the guy.
>
> Then Katie just immediately said, "I need to pray for you." And I said, "All right." She said, "You've got two pins right there?" When I nodded, Katie started to pray, "I judge that witchcraft curse, I judge that serpent activity,

I judge that idolatrous altar in his bloodline that caused this deformity since the day he was born."

As she began to pray for me, it was like the Holy Spirit filled my body. I became hot all over, and after she finished praying for me, the two pins that were on this side, they're gone.

Before, I could only open my mouth to a certain point. But now I can open it wider.[5]

Marquez opened his mouth wide, demonstrating the difference to the cameraman, Steven, who was interviewing him. Then Steven asked, "So you could feel the pins before?"

Marquez replied, "Yeah. And right now, I feel nothing—still nothing! But not only that, man, I just feel different. It's like deep down inside, you know, stuff that's been in my soul for years—hurts, you know, crisis and trauma, things that were done toward me—it's like it just lifted.

"I feel completely, completely different, man. It has affected my faith dramatically, and I want to begin a ministry in here. You know, I want to get in a ministry in here and take it out and all over the world. I want to preach all over the world. I have a healing to talk about, a miracle to tell people about...for the rest of my days."[6]

ACTIVATION

Idolatry is the reason so many people in this world are limping around with canes and are stuck in wheelchairs. I can't tell you how many incredible miracles I've seen manifest in people's bone structures when they renounced idolatry, the curse was broken, and then the serpent was removed.

If you are suffering from any kind of crippling, painful disease or were born with some sort of deformity, pray with me now.

Lord God, I declare that all the trauma in my soul that has let a curse land is being healed by the fire of God. I

decree it's diffusing into my soul right now. I also decree
that Your work on the cross breaks the curse of idolatry
all the way back in my bloodline. By the power of the
exousia authority You have given me, I demand justice
for every birth defect I have suffered from, in Jesus' name.
In agreement with You, Lord God, I judge the crippling,
idolatrous spirits and the work of the serpents that have
been afflicting my body, and I command those crippling
spirits to come out now, in Jesus' name! I command the
serpent to unwind. I also command the spirit of pain to
come out with it, in Jesus' name! Now I command my
dirt body to regenerate bone, muscle, tendons, joints, and
discs, in Jesus' name. Amen.

Now take Communion and speak in firey tongues.

IDOLS, GROWTHS, TUMORS, AND CANCER

Idols, witches, and serpents have their hands in so many pies that
it would be impossible to describe all the afflictions they can place
on the body. This list includes plagues, cancers, tumors, boils, and
even hemorrhoids! As proof I offer this story from 1 Samuel 5.

The Philistines had just stolen the ark of the covenant from the
Israelites. Foolishly they decided to store their highly prized catch
in Ashdod, in the temple of their own god Dagon, right next to
his statue. Unfortunately it didn't end well for the Philistines or
their demon god. The following day they found their idol fallen,
with his face on the ground, bowed down in total obeisance before
the ark of the Lord. Then, believe it or not, the foolish people of
Ashdod set Dagon back up on its feet next to the ark again! The
following day they found him fallen down on his face once more.
This time, however, his head and hands had been broken off by the
judgment of the Lord.

Subsequently all heaven broke loose on the idol-worshipping
Philistines, as the Bible says:

> The hand of the Lord was heavy upon the people of Ashdod, and He caused [mice to spring up and there was] very deadly destruction and He smote the people with [very painful] tumors or boils....But after they had carried {the ark} to Gath, the hand of the Lord was against the city, causing an exceedingly great panic [at the deaths from the plague], for He afflicted the people of the city, both small and great, and tumors or boils broke out on them.
>
> —1 Samuel 5:6, 9

God caused Ashdod to be filled with infected mice, which resulted in a citywide plague. In addition, the people both there and in Gath were covered with tumors and boils, and many of them died. As painful as this must have been, there was also an unusual breakout of hemorrhoids among the citizens. The King James Version of this passage says the Lord smote them with "emerods." *Emerods* is the Hebrew word *tĕchor* (or *t^eḥôrîm*), which according to *Strong's Definitions* means "to burn; a boil or ulcer (from the inflammation), especially a tumor in the anus or pudenda (the piles)."[7] Ouch! This just goes to show that idolatry can be a real pain in the you-know-what!

MIRACLE TESTIMONY

I've seen many cancers, tumors, skin issues, and hemorrhoids get healed when people were delivered from idolatry.

Recently I was in Maine speaking at an event. A woman there had eight tumors on her arm. I simply broke trauma off her and had her renounce idolatry, witchcraft, and serpent activity. Then as I ran my hand across her arm, five of the tumors immediately disappeared—and the remaining ones were much smaller. It took less than thirty seconds for her miracle to manifest itself.

Unfortunately this woman was entirely focused on the three remaining growths, completely ignoring the miracle of the five that had disappeared so quickly. I finally had to take her to her husband to get her to snap out of it. He confirmed that she had had eight growths to start with and that five of them had disappeared. He also agreed with me that the remaining tumors had reduced in size significantly, in fact more than 60 percent! Her pain levels had been significantly reduced as well. And all this after one single, simple prayer!

SNAKE AROUND THE THROAT

Not long ago I was in Turlock, California, for a prayer and healing event with Jennifer Eivaz. A woman who attended received two miracles, the first taking place while she was watching online. Doctors had diagnosed her with a dead vocal cord. At that time I was preaching against the spirit of death. (For more on this topic, read my book *Be Revived*.) As she was listening, I instructed everyone to lay their hands on the areas of their bodies that were giving them trouble. She laid hands on her inactive vocal cord and began to sing; as she did so, she felt it move as it miraculously started working again!

Several months later she attended the next event in person. She told us she had tumors throughout her neck region and all across her chest; they were connected to her lungs. When I looked at her, in the spirit I saw a snake wrapped around her neck, injecting venom into her body. I had her renounce all idolatry, witchcraft, and serpent activity, and then I had her partake of Communion. I released my exousia authority, judged that serpent, and pulled it out of her body.

I then released the Holy Spirit to heal her of all trauma. When I ran my hand across the smaller tumors on her chest, they instantly disappeared with one swipe of my hand. In addition the biggest tumor in her neck shrank significantly and continued to shrink the more she partook of the Communion elements.

CANCER AND THE SERPENTS

Leviathan is a king, making him a strongman over other serpents, which do his bidding. These serpents can cause cancers of every kind, even in the reproductive system. Once we bind the strongman, Leviathan, through a heavenly court order, then we can thoroughly ransack his house, taking up those cancerous snakes. After that, we command the body to vomit out the cancerous venom.

Take another look at Job's rant:

> Let those curse it {the night I was born} who curse the day, who are skilled in rousing up Leviathan....Because it shut not the doors of my mother's womb nor hid sorrow and trouble from my eyes. Why was I not stillborn?... Why did the knees receive me? Or why the breasts, that I should suck?
>
> —JOB 3:8, 10–12

Job was so bitter from the trauma he had endured that he was now releasing witchcraft curses against his life, along with giving permission for Leviathan to carry those curses out. In these verses we also see Job releasing a curse against his mother's breast and womb, desperately wishing he had never been born.

Most cancers, including those on reproductive organs, have witchcraft curses and Leviathan behind them. I vividly recall an encounter at a Tony Kemp meeting where a woman who had undergone a double mastectomy due to breast cancer approached Tony for prayer. Despite the fact she had no remaining breast tissue, the doctors had informed her that the cancer had returned. As Tony ministered to her, he commanded the demonic forces to leave. Simultaneously I witnessed two serpents springing out of her chest.

This incident highlights the insidious nature of these spiritual attacks. Even in the absence of physical breast tissue, the serpents were still at work, causing the recurrence of cancer in her body. I share these experiences not to instill fear but to shed light on the reality of what many people may still be unaware of.

MIRACLE TESTIMONY

Through a phone call I once ministered to a woman who was battling breast cancer. Before the call I had a vision of a sickbed covered with cheetah skins. Cheetahs are the fastest land animal in the world, so I knew this signified it was going to be a quick healing.

During our conversation the woman shared details of the numerous traumas she had experienced in her life, confessing they had made her bitter, even causing her to engage in witchcraft. She had repented of these things, but she felt they still might be contributing factors.

She then gave me details concerning the breast tumor, which was the size and hardness of a baseball. It also had been leaking foul-smelling, toxic secretions for many years. Thankfully she had been listening to my healing soaker *Sons of the Light*, and as a result the tumor had started to collapse, forming a moonlike crater in the center. It was still painful, though, as the edges of the crater were dry with crusty ridges.

I started by praying against the trauma in her soul. Then I opened a case in the heavenly court, releasing my exousia authority on her behalf. I had her renounce all idolatry, witchcraft, and serpents. I then broke the witchcraft curse that Leviathan was carrying out on her breast, decreeing that he was a fugitive from the law. Next we prayed in fiery tongues as I commanded those spirits to come out by court decree, in the name of Jesus. Then we took Communion, decreeing that the serpent's head was being crushed. Finally I commanded her dirt body to vomit out the cancerous venom and the breast tissue to regenerate.

She reported instantly feeling as if she was covered with fire. She also felt a lot of movement in her breast. When she checked, the tumor had already shrunk in size by at least 40 percent. Plus, instead of the breast flesh looking necrotic, it had turned a healthy-looking pink, as it was coming back to life. Along with all this the woman said she felt totally different in her soul.

Over the next few days I checked on her progress via text message. The tumor was continuing to collapse; the hard, crusty edges were getting softer; and new breast tissue was forming. She also wrote that for five days after we prayed, yellow fluid drained out of her breast that, as she put it, looked like "snake venom."

PROSTATE CANCER MIRACLE TESTIMONY

This revelation is not just for women but also for men. Last year Dog the Bounty Hunter; his wife, Francie; and I traveled to Parchman Prison in Mississippi to minister to the men there. One inmate, Ralph, had been diagnosed with prostate cancer. It was extremely difficult for him to use the bathroom due to swelling. The facility had been giving him medication for six months in an attempt to alleviate some of the pain and discomfort while he waited to go to an outside doctor for more involved treatment.

I came early to the event so I could pray for people. When I called for those with cancer to come up front, Ralph had already said to other inmates, "I ain't letting no woman lay hands on me." Fortunately, his friends pushed him to receive prayer, which he finally did. As he approached, he told me the swelling the prostate cancer caused made it very painful for him to walk.

I prayed a simple prayer based on the biblical precepts you have learned in this book. First, I laid hands on him, releasing the Holy Spirit to minister to any trauma or wounds in his soul. Then I asked him to renounce any idolatry, witchcraft, or serpent activity in his life. I released a judicial decree from heaven against those spirits, declaring he was under grace, not the law, and then commanded those spirits to come out. I also spoke to his dirt body, commanding it to vomit out the cancer and for the Holy Spirit to quicken his mortal body unto regeneration.

Immediately he clasped his pelvic area and said he'd just felt something burst inside him! (I believe it was the pocket of cancer.)

The next thing I knew, he was jumping up and down, dancing around in circles. Out of the blue he then took off running around the gym! (Remember, he had just been experiencing severe pain simply from walking forward for prayer.) When he returned, out of breath, I asked how he was feeling, and he shouted, "It's gone! I feel it—I feel it!" When I asked how he knew, he just kept shouting, "I feel it!" over and over.

The next day my media team interviewed him. He was full of excitement because of the miracle that had taken place in his body. All the pain and swelling were gone, and he could use the bathroom without any problems. At the end of the interview he took off running around the chapel again, unprompted. God is so good! [8]

ACTIVATION

Now it's time for us to activate our own faith. Are you ready? Let's begin by praying this prayer:

> *Father, in the mighty name of Jesus, I stand before Your holy court, renouncing idolatry, witchcraft, and all serpent activity. I decree that I am completely forgiven of every sin, including bitterness that any idols, witches, Leviathan, and other serpents have been using to curse my breasts, my reproductive organs, and any other part of my body. I thank You, Lord, that You are now passing judgment on the serpent because all accusations against me are covered by the precious blood of Jesus.*
>
> *I also decree that I firmly stand in Your grace for every place I broke the law with my idolatry. Jesus fulfilled the righteous requirement of the law on my behalf—something I could never do on my own. As Your Word declares, "All have sinned and fall short of the glory of God, and are justified by his grace as a gift, through the redemption that is in Christ Jesus" (Rom. 3:23–24, ESV).*

Now take Communion, and decree that the serpent's head is being crushed and that your soul is being healed of all trauma. Decree that your soul is nourished, refreshed, and strengthened by the blood of Jesus.

When you are ready, continue by saying these words:

Lord, I invite the fire of God to flow from the judicial bench of the Ancient of Days to burn up every bit of chaff in my soul that I may have in common with this assignment, including pride and bitterness. As the fire burns away any remaining chaff within my soul and consumes every wicked internal foe, the briars and thorns in my spiritual vineyard are being utterly incinerated.

Now I invoke my exousia authority to release the power of judicial decisions against this serpent. I decree that they are fugitives from the law because they are carrying out a curse against me. Jesus has already become a curse on my behalf, so this curse is illegal, and I break it now in Jesus' name. I now release a judicial decision against every witchcraft spirit, every idol, and every serpent that is causing cancer in my body in Jesus' name. By heavenly court order they are arrested and restrained from committing any further harm against me.

Now, Father, I take up this serpent and pull it out of every area of my body in which it is causing cancer, and I cast it into the fire, declaring, "Burn and do not return."

Now I command my dirt body to vomit out the cancerous venom of the serpent. Tumors and growths, you must now drain, dissolve, and exit my body in the mighty name of Jesus. I also command the regeneration of new, healthy flesh. In Jesus' name, amen.

CHAPTER 10

FERTILITY AND FOOD

Be fruitful and multiply, and fill the earth....Every moving
thing that lives shall be food for you; I give you every-
thing, as I gave you the green plants and vegetables.
—GENESIS 9:1, 3 AMP

L ET'S TALK ABOUT reproductive issues, food addictions, gout, arthritis, and more. Just as Leviathan curses the breast and the womb with cancer, it also brings about a wide variety of reproductive issues, including infertility and miscarriages. As you will see when it comes to problems in the reproductive system, idolatry, witchcraft, and infertility are directly connected.

A perfect example is the story of Rachel and Jacob and their continuous struggle to build their family. There was constant competition between Rachel and her sister, Leah, to produce offspring for their shared husband, Jacob—with Rachel on the losing end. Although Jacob loved Rachel more, Leah was by far the more fertile wife, bearing seven children for him. Rachel bore only two

natural sons, and that after an epic struggle. She even died during
the birth of her second son, Benjamin.

What was the original source behind Rachel's battle against
infertility? Scripture proves that she had put her faith in the pagan
practices of idolatry and witchcraft to try to successfully conceive.
We see evidence of this throughout her marriage to Jacob.

RACHEL AND THE MANDRAKES

In her twisted belief system Rachel dabbled in witchcraft in an
effort to get pregnant. Genesis 30 tells the story of Rachel desperately putting her faith in the power of a mandrake (a plant) instead
of God to fulfill her dream of being a mother:

> Now Reuben went at the time of wheat harvest and found
> some mandrakes (love apples) in the field and brought
> them to his mother Leah. Then Rachel said to Leah, Give
> me, I pray you, some of your son's mandrakes.
>
> But [Leah] answered, Is it not enough that you have
> taken my husband without your taking away my son's
> mandrakes also? And Rachel said, Jacob shall sleep with
> you tonight [in exchange] for your son's mandrakes.
>
> And Jacob came out of the field in the evening, and
> Leah went out to meet him and said, You must sleep with
> me [tonight], for I have certainly paid your hire with my
> son's mandrakes. So he slept with her that night.
>
> And God heeded Leah's [prayer], and she conceived
> and bore Jacob [her] fifth son.
>
> —GENESIS 30:14–17

The mandrake, also called "Satan's apple," is a plant whose long,
thick taproot resembles the human body. Mandrakes have long
been associated with magic, witchcraft, and the supernatural. In
fact, although these plants are no longer in common use, herbal
mandrake is still studied by people who are interested in the occult.
According to biblical and historical writings, mandrakes were

believed to cause fertility, and they were used in a variety of magic rituals, from love spells to divination.[1]

The story of Leah and Rachel verbally wrestling over the mandrake plants is one of pure insanity and a reliance on witchcraft. Rachel was so sure she could tap into the magical powers of the mandrakes to help her conceive that she even traded Leah a night with their mutual husband to obtain them. Well, her plan totally backfired, as it was Leah, not Rachel, who got pregnant.

RACHEL'S IDOLS

Many gods of ancient times falsely promised youth and fertility to their worshippers. The opposite was actually true, with many of their followers becoming infertile and barren. Regrettably Rachel was one of these followers. She stubbornly held on to her gods, believing their lies, and unfortunately I believe they were a source of her struggle to get pregnant.

Throughout their marriage Jacob had often been cheated out of his fair share of the family wealth by Leah and Rachel's father, Laban. Laban recognized the favor of God that was resting on Jacob, and he used that favor to increase his own flocks and herds. Throughout the many years of Jacob's labor, Laban barely rewarded him, treating him more like a hired hand than a valued business partner and family member. Finally, tired of it, Jacob and his wives fled Laban's camps in the dead of night with their children, flocks, and herds.

Sadly, as they snuck away, Rachel secretly stole the household gods that belonged to her father (Gen. 31:19)—likely the physical idols and images of gods worshipped by the pagans of that region, including their fertility gods. (This proves that Laban, Leah, Rachel, and their entire family were idol worshippers.) After they fled, Laban caught up to them, angry about the theft of his idols. Unaware of what his wife Rachel had done, Jacob gave Laban permission to fully search his camp. But still not willing to let go of these prized possessions, Rachel concealed the idols beneath her

camel's saddle. She literally sat on the stolen goods; then when her
father questioned her, she claimed she was unable to move because
she was experiencing her monthly menstruation.

Why would Rachel go to such great lengths to abscond with
her father's idols, then concoct a story to keep them hidden? She
had struggled throughout her entire marriage to bear children for
Jacob—and later, she even perished while birthing her second son,
Benjamin. Obviously she had mistakenly relied on the false promises of those fertility gods instead of the power of the one true God
to help her conceive.

GOD'S MERCY

Even in all these things, when God granted Rachel her desire to
bear children with Jacob, it was an indication of His mercy toward
her, despite her insistence on clinging to her family's pagan tradi-
tions. The Bible says this:

> Then God remembered Rachel and answered her pleading
> and *made it possible for her to have children.* And [now for
> the first time] she became pregnant and bore a son; and
> she said, *God has taken away my reproach, disgrace, and
> humiliation.*
> —GENESIS 30:22–23, EMPHASIS ADDED

This shows us that Rachel's conceptions were a gift from the
Lord, not from idols or the use of mandrakes! God removed not
only the humiliation of her barrenness but also the reproach and
disgrace of her practice of witchcraft and idolatry.

THE SERPENT CARRIES OUT THE CURSE

Idolatry and witchcraft create a place for curses to land. Remember
Job's acrimonious rant in which he released a curse against his
mother's breasts and womb in a desperate wish to prevent his own

birth (Job 3:10–12)? Again, in his ancient wisdom Job knew that Leviathan was the one that carried out those witchcraft curses (v. 8).

Leviathan is also frequently responsible for barrenness, stillbirths, and miscarriages. In the midst of his grief, Job declared, "Indeed, let that night be barren; let no shout of joy penetrate it!" (v. 7, NET), and "Why was I not stillborn? Why did I not give up the ghost when my mother bore me?...Or [why] was I not a miscarriage, hidden and put away, as infants who never saw light?" (vv. 11, 16).

Job made these frightening statements right after he made it clear that Leviathan is the one that executes the witchcraft curses. If you are battling infertility, barrenness, or a propensity toward miscarriages or stillbirths, it could be witchcraft, idolatry, and Leviathan at play, working together against your fertility. In fact this terrible trio has their hands in all kinds of reproductive issues and disorders, as you will see in the following testimonies.

MIRACLE TESTIMONY

A woman in Seattle reported having severe endometriosis, which is a disease in which tissue similar to the lining of the uterus grows outside the uterus. It can cause severe pain in the pelvis region, and it makes it very difficult to get pregnant.

This woman also suffered from scar tissue in her bowels and surrounding areas in her body. She said the pain from both of these problems was extreme and getting worse; it persistently shot all the way up her back and down to her knees.

As I was praying for the removal of serpents in the general meeting, she said all pain suddenly left her body. However, she decided not to say anything yet; she wanted to wait until the next day to confirm she had experienced a real miracle. Interestingly enough, she had been bitten by a real snake while in Florida the previous year. Even though the bite had left a bad scar on her body, it eventually healed on its own. As she shared her testimony with all of us, she said that when I prayed against the serpents, it changed her life forever.

INFECTIONS AND SERPENTS

I often see infections die off in people's bodies once they are de-snakified. This includes areas in the female reproductive system. One woman reported a revealing story that proves this point. While she was listening to my teaching on serpents, the Lord showed her a demonic snake that had been attacking her with an infection in a specific private area of her body. The infection had persisted for many years—not only causing physical pain and discomfort but also affecting her on a deeply personal level.

As she was soaking during my teaching—and beginning to drift off to sleep—she suddenly had a vision of a snake staring at her, its mouth open. Startled, she immediately rose up and did as Jesus said, taking up that serpent and throwing it into the abyss, commanding it to burn and never return.

When I asked whether she could feel a change in that part of her body, she responded that she could definitely feel a great difference. She knew beyond a shadow of a doubt that she had been healed.

CERVICAL MIRACLE AND OTHER TESTIMONIES

Another woman shared an amazing encounter she experienced while in a meeting I was holding in Seattle. During the afternoon session a woman who was sitting behind this woman had a vision of her pelvic area bursting into flames and saw a snake coming out of her body. The person who had the vision had no idea that this woman was scheduled to undergo surgery in three weeks to have her cervix and a hernia removed.

After she shared her testimony, I asked whether she felt any difference in that part of her body. She replied that she had been feeling an enormous amount of pain for over four weeks—but now it was totally gone!

So many people have also reported to me of miscarriages being avoided and of longed-for pregnancies finally being conceived, all after serpents were removed from their wombs and forbidden to return. These and multiple other testimonies prove that many fertility problems are rooted in witchcraft curses being activated by Leviathan or other serpents—and when they are removed and cast into fire, the problems are resolved.

ACTIVATION

Because so many reproductive issues have idols, witchcraft, and serpents behind them, I want to emphasize the importance of discerning and addressing any potential idols that could bring these witchcraft curses into your life. Let's take a moment right now to identify and judge these idols, which may be connected to your bloodline. Remember, the idols Rachel clung to were rooted in her family and their history of worshipping them. Additionally, Rachel's desire for these idols was so strong that after she stole them from her father's house, she went to great lengths to hide them, even lying to her own father to cover the theft. She was unaware that the idols she was worshipping—and likely praying to in order to conceive a child—were probably the very cause of her infertility. In your own life it is important that you uncover any idols you have created, whether they come from your family line or not, once and for all.

Take out the Communion elements, and obey Paul's admonishment in 1 Corinthians 11:28 to examine yourself before you partake. Don't forget to decree that your soul is becoming nourished, refreshed, and strengthened as you eat and drink of the Communion elements so you will be healed of all the effects of trauma, bitterness, pride, gossip, offense, and any other sin connected to idols, witchcraft, and serpents. Then decree that every curse is broken by the power of the cross and that the head of the serpent is crushed.

Now, if you're dealing with an infection, fibroids, excessive cramping, bleeding, a propensity toward miscarriages, barrenness, debilitating symptoms of menopause, or any other issue within your reproductive system, let's pray together right now.

Speak these words:

> *Lord Jesus, I stand before the court of heaven, repenting for any involvement with idolatry, witchcraft, and serpentine activity. As I testify here, I decree that I will overcome the enemy by the blood of the Lamb and my testimony in this court.*
>
> *I renounce idolatry, witchcraft, and any serpent activity in my life, and I decree I'm under grace and not the law. Wherever my sin in these areas has increased and abounded, Your grace has superabounded all the more over it. I decree that I have been made upright and am in right standing with You through Your freely given grace. This grace causes me to be justified, acquitted of all charges the enemy has brought against me.*
>
> *Father, in the name of Jesus, I ask that the wheels of fire on the judicial bench of the Ancient of Days would go back in time, through my bloodline, to where the curses came into my life in the first place, and burn them up at the root. I also command the fiery judgment of this court to stream forth from the judicial bench to drive every serpent in my body out of hiding, just as the fire did for the apostle Paul.*
>
> *I also pray for a new baptism of the Holy Spirit and fire to fill me. Lord, burn away all the chaff in my soul with Your unquenchable fire. I decree that the wicked internal foe is being burned up now as Your holy fire entirely infuses my inner being.*

Now spend some time praying in fiery tongues, as well as singing along to a fire song. Then speak these words:

> *I judge and curse the root of trauma. I command it to leave in the name of Jesus. I command the spirit of trauma, as well as the spirit of grief, disappointment, and sorrow—stemming from barrenness, the inability to conceive,*

reproductive issues, and the relentless curses that have been placed on my body—to come out now in the name of Jesus.

I break the curse of barrenness, stillbirth, and miscarriage now in the name of Jesus. I release a divine judgment against Leviathan from the court of heaven for carrying out curses against me. I decree that every curse pronounced over me is illegal because Jesus already became a curse for me. Thus, this court pronounces judgment on you, Leviathan, right now. I exercise my exousia authority and power to render judicial decisions against you for every place you have cursed me in my reproductive organs or system. I arrest you by heavenly court decree and declare that the curses are broken, in Jesus' name! I also release a restraining order against you, Leviathan, to prevent you from continuing to attack me from this point on, in Jesus' name. I also command every spirit working with Leviathan to come out now, in Jesus' name!

Prepare the Communion elements again.

Now I address tumors, fibroids, infections, diseases of the reproductive system, bleeding issues, infertility, barrenness, a propensity toward miscarriages and stillbirths, debilitating symptoms of menopause, and all reproduction problems.

As I partake of the Bread of Life, I speak to my dirt body, commanding it to expel every issue, in Jesus' name. I command every problem in my reproductive system to be dissolved, sweat out, urinated out, and evacuated completely, in Jesus' name. I also command my body to absorb the life-giving power of the Bread of Life and the Holy Spirit quickening my mortal flesh, in the name of Jesus. I command my cells, organs, and every part of my reproduction system to regenerate, and I decree the restoration of all my flesh, in Jesus' name!

I declare fertility enters my body right now. I decree that I will conceive and that I will carry the pregnancy to full term—resulting in a perfectly formed, perfectly healthy baby. In the name of Jesus, amen!

I also judge and bind up every menopausal symptom, in Jesus' name, including hot flashes, night sweats, and mood swings. I judge them all! I cast out every diabolical spirit behind those symptoms now, in Jesus' name. I loose the life-giving Spirit of the Holy Ghost to regenerate and quicken my mortal body until perfect health and hormonal balance are achieved and normalized, in Jesus' name!

Now partake of the elements and worship the Lord.

THE SERPENT AND FOOD

If you are struggling with food-related issues, there could also be a snake at the root of the problem. Recall that the very first manifestation of a demonic serpent was when Satan himself entered the garden and weaponized *food* against Eve and then Adam—and his deception caused all of humankind to fall.

> And He {God} said, Who told you that you were naked? Have you eaten of the tree of which I commanded you that you should not eat? And the man said, The woman whom You gave to be with me—she gave me [fruit] from the tree, and I ate. And the Lord God said to the woman, What is this you have done? And the woman said, The serpent beguiled (cheated, outwitted, and deceived) me, and I ate.
>
> —GENESIS 3:11–13

From the beginning that old serpent has used food to drive humans to sin. In fact the snake's strategy to leverage food against humankind was so effective that it caused *everyone* to fall into darkness and demonic control from that point on.

Food is still the serpent's number one weapon that he utilizes to steal from, kill, and destroy human beings. Every single person on the planet has to eat to survive. So, what better tool for the enemy to manipulate and turn against us than that which we cannot live without?

It is shocking how many ways the serpent has used food to control, ultimately harm, and even kill the people of this world. In an effort to twist the healthy nutrition found in our planet's food supply, an insidious agenda is currently underway. In the United States multiple meat- and food-processing plants have suddenly and mysteriously burned to the ground.[2] Recently, the US Food and Drug Administration and the US Department of Agriculture approved lab-grown meats for consumption in restaurants and for selling in grocery stores.[3] These products are touted as extremely healthy and good for the human body. However, scientific testing has already proven that is not true, and they could, in fact, be very harmful to people.[4]

There is also a systematic attack being released to put small local farmers out of business as more genetically modified organisms (GMOs) and pesticide-based producers take their place. Wealthy individuals with hidden agendas are also buying up farmland to use for their own insidious purposes. Even a new campaign to brainwash the public into eating insects as our main protein source has been launched and touted in the liberal media.[5] This is all part of the agenda of the serpent to trick us into eating from the wrong tree—again.

"Eating from the wrong tree" causes sickness and even death. Did you know that more people die of food and obesity-related diseases than of cancer?[6] Toxic food and obesity can cause heart disease, high blood pressure, diabetes, high cholesterol levels, infertility, and chronic pain—and that is just a small fraction of the list.

A study published in *The BMJ* concluded that a rapid rise in the consumption of "ultra-processed" food and drink could be a leading cause of obesity and food-related diseases.[7] An earlier study showed that 58 percent of our daily calories come from these types of foods, and another 21 percent comes from the added sugars, which have been proven to cause cancer.[8] Ultra-processed foods are those whose original natural ingredients have been so overly processed that the final product is totally void of any nutritional value. Food manufacturers use artificial flavors, colors, sweeteners, stabilizers, and other additives to mask their undesirable qualities and make them taste like real food. Processed breads, cakes, cookies, pies, and salty snacks are just a few examples of some of the foods in this category—all demonic delicacies the serpent coaxes us to daily consume.

Because over half of our daily calorie intake consists of these foods, our bodies are left severely malnourished and deficient of the nutrients needed for healthy cell growth and resistance to disease. A 2016 newspaper article said that ultra-processed foods can make people overweight or obese. That, in turn, sets them up for serious health problems like type 2 diabetes, heart disease, stroke, and cancer.[9]

What would make us *choose* to eat something that does not bring health and vitality to our bodies—and can even cause disease and death? From the beginning that old snake in the garden tempted Adam and Eve to eat food that God said they were not supposed to eat, food that proved to be fatal to them, and all of humanity faced death as a result.

Satan accomplished this deception by appealing to Adam and Eve's hungry souls. Let me unpack this for you, starting here:

> And the Lord God formed man of the slime of the earth: and breathed into his face the breath of life, and man became a living soul.
>
> —GENESIS 2:7, DRA

Adam and Eve were created as living souls. Watch how the serpent specifically used delicious-looking food to then tempt Eve's soul:

> And when the woman saw that the tree was good for
> food, and that it was pleasant to the eyes, and a tree to
> be desired to make one wise, she took of the fruit thereof,
> and did eat, and gave also unto her husband with her;
> and he did eat.
>
> —GENESIS 3:6, KJV

This verse says Eve "saw" the fruit, and it was pleasant to her "eyes." The eyes are the windows to the soul. When she saw the food, it was her soul that was tempted to take it and eat it, even though God had told them not to do that very thing. This scripture also says she "desired" the tree and its fruit. According to the Bible, your passions and desires come from your soul.

Did you know that *nephesh*, the Hebrew word translated as "soul" in Genesis 2:7 (DRA), can also be translated as "appetite"?[10] This means that countless people are overeating and/or consuming nutritionally deficient foods because they are *more than* physically hungry. The population of the entire world is living in a chronic state of being wounded. We usually don't overeat because we need more physical nourishment. (Unless the food we are eating doesn't contain any real sustenance. Then our bodies will still be hungry because we are not eating enough true nourishment.) Rather, many times we overeat because our souls are wounded and we are desperate to be comforted, to find relief from the pain we are enduring.

The souls of people are hungry today. Inside every human being is the desire to be consoled, loved, fulfilled, appreciated, respected, and satisfied and to experience joy and happiness. When those needs aren't met, our souls become hungry. And then, unfortunately, we tend to fill our mental and emotional starvation through addictions to money, sex, bad entertainment, and, yes, even overeating.

Food can bring a false, temporary sense of comfort and satisfaction. Food is supposed to meet an important need in our lives for nutrition—and healthy comfort. But too much of a good thing often ends in condemnation and shame, especially as the pounds pack on.

Unfortunately many people also use food to self-medicate their internal pain until food literally becomes an idol in their lives that they run to for comfort.

FOOD OFFERED TO IDOLS

Virtually every ancient idolatrous ceremony included offering food to idols. Idol worshippers would dedicate their food sacrifices to demon gods and then consume that devoted food. In doing so, they believed they would become one with the demons they venerated, enabling them to partake of their demonic power. Consequently idolaters would feast lavishly on the food they sacrificed to those evil spirits.

The apostle Paul said something eye-opening about this practice in his first letter to the Corinthians:

> Do not be worshipers of false gods as some of them were, as it is written, The people sat down to eat and drink [the sacrifices offered to the golden calf at Horeb] and rose to sport (to dance and give way to jesting and hilarity).
> —1 CORINTHIANS 10:7

Paul warned us to not partake in any kind of worship of false gods (v. 14), as the Israelites did, including participating in the feasts and immoral revelry that honored those idols.

Later in the chapter, Paul added this shocking admonition:

> What do I imply then? That food offered to idols is [intrinsically changed by the fact and amounts to] anything or that an idol itself is a [living] thing? No, I am suggesting that what the pagans sacrifice they offer [in effect] to demons (to evil spiritual powers) and not to God [at all]. *I do not want you to fellowship and be partners with diabolical spirits [by eating at their feasts].*
> —1 CORINTHIANS 10:19–20, EMPHASIS ADDED

Here, Paul indicates that a person can come into "fellowship and be partners with" demonic spirits "by eating at their feasts." Excessive eating and drinking was a form of worship the ancients practiced to become one with their demon gods. It's the same today; nothing has changed.

Demons are accustomed to having food sacrificed to them! So, to get their fix, those spirits will drive you to overeat, even when you're not hungry. They will tempt you to consume junk food and sugary sodas and drinks that will cause you to gain weight and increase your likelihood of developing diabetes, high blood pressure, and high cholesterol. Every time you acquiesce to their temptations by overeating and consuming food that is nutritionally compromised, you are offering a food sacrifice to those demons, thus partnering with them "by eating at their feasts."

When you turn food into an idol to comfort and medicate your soul pain, you are inviting demons to attack every part of your life, including your physical body. This is why the Jerusalem Council instructed the Gentile believers to "abstain from meats offered to idols" (Acts 15:29, KJV). Certain bad eating habits will create demonic attachments.

COMMUNION DISSOLVES THE PARTNERSHIP WITH DEMONS

In the same chapter we cited previously, the apostle Paul also taught on the most powerful remedy in the universe that will enable you to escape this demonic food trap: Communion.

Right before Paul warned believers never to fellowship with diabolical spirits by eating at their feasts, he taught on the power of fellowshipping with Christ's body and blood to overcome idols. Let's look at what he wrote:

> Therefore, my dearly beloved, shun (keep clear away from, avoid by flight if need be) any sort of idolatry (of loving or venerating anything more than God)....The cup of

blessing [of wine at the Lord's Supper] upon which we ask
[God's] blessing, does it not mean [that in drinking it] *we
participate in and share a fellowship (a communion) in the
blood of Christ* (the Messiah)? The bread which we break,
does it not mean [that in eating it] *we participate in and
share a fellowship (a communion) in the body of Christ?*
—1 CORINTHIANS 10:14, 16, EMPHASIS ADDED

Paul begins this section of Scripture by warning believers never
to be involved in idolatry of any sort. He even urgently commands
us to shun it, to flee from it at all costs! Then he gives the antidote
that will empower us to break our agreement with idolatry. What
is this antidote? The "fellowship" that comes with partaking of the
body and the blood of Jesus! This is only a few verses before he
describes the fellowship and partnership people form with demons
by eating at their feasts.

Do you see the comparison Paul presents here? Drinking of the
cup (representing Christ's blood) and eating the bread (symbolizing
His body) of Communion cause you to *fellowship* with the sacrificed Christ! In other words, partaking of the Lord's Supper breaks
any fellowship you may have created with demons by feasting at
their table.

Yes, as you draw near to the Lord, celebrating His great, all-
encompassing sacrifice, you enter into deep fellowship with Him.
This breaks your agreement and partnership with the "food gods"
and halts their ability to drive you to eat from the wrong tree.

YOU WILL NEVER HUNGER OR THIRST

Communion has the power to heal your soul of its need for comfort and even quenches your unholy appetites. Jesus said this about
His body and blood:

I am the Bread of Life. He who comes to Me will never be
hungry, and he who believes in and cleaves to and trusts

in and relies on Me will never thirst any more (at any
time).

—John 6:35

As we noted in chapter 5, the word *thirst* here (Greek *dipsaō*)
refers to "those...who painfully feel their want of, and eagerly
long for, those things by which the soul is refreshed, supported,
strengthened."[11]

When your soul is wounded, you can feel the pain radiating
from your inner being as it begins to control and destroy your
entire life. That creates a desperate desire and an eager need to seek
relief for your soul. Again, that's why many of us reach for food to
satisfy a need inside us we barely realize is there. Here, conversely,
Jesus said you can reach for the most powerful nourishment in the
world: the life and soul-healing power of His body and His blood,
which will quench that unholy yearning. As you partake of His
"drink"—His blood—you will never thirst again because your soul
will be refreshed, supported, and strengthened.

Likewise, when you partake of the Bread—His body—you will
never "hunger" (Greek *peinaō*), which means "to crave ardently."[12]
Eating of the life-giving bread will not only cease the cravings of
your soul but also extinguish your cravings for foods that bring
destruction to your body! Jesus said, "For My flesh is true and genuine food, and My blood is true and genuine drink" (John 6:55).
Christ's body and blood provide real nourishment for your physical
body that can take away any fleshly hankering for sugary treats
and junk food in the late-night hours.

I challenge you to reach for His table every time a craving
hits—*before* you "break weak" and run to the fridge! If you will
stop and make a decree, using these scriptures, and then partake
of His sacrifice through Communion, you will find yourself completely satisfied and no longer needing that evil snack.

Activation

If you are suffering with food-related issues, possibly even controlled by food, then please prepare the elements of Communion for this activation in the Spirit.

Speak these powerful words aloud:

> Lord Jesus, as I partake of Your body and Your blood, I first ask that my soul would be healed of any wound that has caused me to reach toward food for comfort. Fill my soul with Your power and Your life so that my inner being is refreshed, nourished, and strengthened. I decree that I will never hunger or thirst for the wrong things again, because I am eating of Your flesh and drinking Your blood, which bring health and nourishment to me, body, soul, and spirit.
>
> I also take in the power of Your sacrifice, which breaks the fellowship and partnership I created with diabolical spirits by eating at their feasts. I repent for sitting and partaking at that demonic table by overeating, by consuming the wrong kinds of food, and even by eating when I wasn't hungry. I repent of turning food into an idol. I ask Your forgiveness for every time I feasted at the table of demons, bringing food sacrifices to them. I decree that as I meditate on You and celebrate what You accomplished for me through Your sacrifice, I am fellowshipping with You and Your body and blood. Thus, the power of Your blood, shed on the cross, is breaking any fellowship and partnership I made with these demonic gods.
>
> I also decree that I am under grace and not the law. You have paid the price for all my sins on the cross of Calvary, and I accept the grace that is legally mine now, in Your name.
>
> Now, as I partake of Your body and blood, I decree that the power of the cross is crushing the head of that old serpent that shipwrecked all humanity by successfully

tempting them with food. I decree that he will no longer have the power to tempt me with food, because of what You accomplished at Calvary! I decree that from this moment on, no demon can control me, drive me to eat, or cause me to gain weight or make me sick with any food-related diseases because of the power of the cross! I also decree that Your body is real food and Your blood is real drink, so when I take it in, I don't hunger anymore. I decree that the Lord's Supper has the power to remove every unhealthy food craving that tries to take over my mind or my soul, in Your name!

Now partake of Communion. If you suffer from any food-related disorders, list them now. Put them under the power of the cross, and cast them out of your body now, in Jesus' name! Keep taking Communion on a daily basis until you achieve the total breakthrough.

GOUT AND THE SERPENT

Gout is a "common and complex form of arthritis" that is "characterized by sudden, severe attacks of pain, swelling, redness and tenderness in one or more joints, most often in the big toe."[13]

Gout is caused by a buildup of a substance called uric acid in the blood. If you produce too much uric acid or your kidneys don't effectively filter it out, it can cause tiny, sharp crystals to form in and around the joints, which then cause them to become inflamed and extremely painful.

"An attack of gout can occur suddenly, often waking you up in the middle of the night with the sensation that your big toe [or other joint] is on fire." The affected area gets so hot, swollen, and tender that even a bedsheet touching it may seem unbearable.[14]

Though gout frequently affects the big toe, it can also occur in joints like the ankles, knees, elbows, wrists, and fingers. The pain, extremely severe for several hours, can linger to some degree up to a few weeks. Gout can also restrict your range of motion.[15]

The first time I ever connected gout to a demonic serpent attack was when a friend of mine, Russel, experienced a miraculous deliverance and healing. Russel had been suffering from painful gout for twenty years. In fact it ran through his entire family; his father, as well as his uncles and brothers, suffered from it.

Russel attended a local event in Arizona in which I was teaching about serpents and the fire of God. The event was powerful, with everyone pressing into the fiery presence of the Lord. Later that night, as Russel slept, he had a vision of a sea snake wrapped around his foot.

Upon performing some research, Russel discovered that the sea snake is one of the most venomous serpents in the world. A nocturnal hunter, this serpent can camouflage itself, and it will search in the crevices of coral reefs to find its prey, swim backward or remain motionless, and then ambush the unsuspecting fish that try to shelter underneath it.[16]

When Russel shared this information with me, I didn't even need to interpret its meaning to him. He knew this serpent was behind the nighttime attacks of pain and swelling he had suffered all those years from gout. He also understood, through spiritual revelation, that the uric acid causing the gout was actually the highly toxic venom of the sea snake. Since that serpent had advanced camouflage technology, Russel didn't realize he had been carrying it around for decades.

Russel did as Jesus said His followers would do and took up that serpent, throwing it into the fiery abyss. He hasn't had an attack of gout since.

BALTIMORE MIRACLE TESTIMONY

As I mentioned earlier, I was at a women's conference in Baltimore, Maryland. When I entered the sanctuary, I saw a man moving chairs around but simultaneously holding up his right arm. I then saw in the spirit a serpent wrapped around his limb.

When I approached him to ask what was wrong, he said he was experiencing a flare-up of gout and rheumatoid arthritis from which he had suffered for twenty-three years. These problems caused him excruciating pain. I told him it was because he had a snake wrapped around his arm. He looked shocked, to say the least, but when I offered to pray for him, he didn't hesitate.

His arm was very swollen and extremely stiff, and it had quite a few large knots on it. I first prayed for his soul to be healed of trauma; then I took that serpent to court. I released fire, then pulled the serpent off his arm. Immediately, the swelling and pain went down 50 percent.

I suggested we take Communion while I prayed for him a second time, to which he wholeheartedly agreed. As we partook of the elements, I decreed that we were doing so in remembrance of Christ's work on the cross, where He crushed the serpent's head. Next I commanded the man's dirt body to vomit out the venom of the serpent, the uric acid, and to receive the life-giving power of the body of Christ. I then rebuked the rheumatoid arthritis, casting it out in Jesus' name.

The swelling instantly reduced even more—so much so that he was able to bend his wrist and move his fingers, which he couldn't do before. Also, the large knots on his arm shrank significantly.

The next day I sought him out to inquire of his status. He said that since I had prayed, he had been experiencing a strange sensation in his hand. It was tingling, and he could envision something like maggots eating all the toxins coming out of his hand and going up his arm.

When I asked, he said his pain level before the prayer had been a ten out of ten, but now he had zero pain! He ended his testimony by saying, "I am pain-free, and I believe in my heart that since you prayed for me, I am free of gout, 100 percent."

ACTIVATION

If you are suffering from gout or any form of arthritis, go ahead and prepare the elements of Communion for this activation in the Spirit.

Speak these powerful words aloud:

> *Lord Jesus, I thank You for Your body and Your blood. I thank You for Your work on the cross of Calvary that crushed the head of the serpent. I take in the power of Your sacrifice, and I repent for any partnership I may have had with demons, witchcraft, or idolatry. Because of Your sacrifice on the cross, I decree that I am under grace and not the law. You have paid the price for all my sins on the cross of Calvary, and I accept the grace that is legally mine now, in Your name.*
>
> *Now as I partake of Your body and blood, I decree that the power of the cross is crushing the head of any serpent that is in my body. I also pray for the fire of the Holy Spirit within me to fill me. Lord, burn away all the chaff in my soul with Your unquenchable fire, and drive any serpent that is present out of my body. Any venom associated with those serpents that is in my body I command to come out now, in the name of Jesus.*

Now partake of Communion. If you suffer from any form of arthritis or gout, put it under the power of the cross, and cast it out of your body now, in Jesus' name!

THE REPTILIAN BRAIN

The basal ganglia are a group of structures deep in the center of the brain that play a crucial role. Responsible for motor control, motor learning, and various cognitive processes and bodily functions, their presence in the body is vital for managing the simplest everyday tasks.

Interestingly the basal ganglia have sometimes been referred to as the "reptilian brain." Why? Because it was once thought that the basal ganglia, rather than more-complex brain structures, were prominent in the brains of all reptiles, including serpents.[17]

When the basal ganglia are damaged or impaired, it can lead to neurodegenerative disorders such as Parkinson's disease, dementia, Huntington's disease, and Alzheimer's disease, along with sleeping disorders and other conditions like restless leg syndrome.

I personally experienced restless leg syndrome for a couple of months. It came on me seemingly out of nowhere. When I asked the Lord to show me the cause, I received a vision of a snake wrapped around my basal ganglia—my reptilian brain. As soon as I removed it, the restless leg problem ceased.

I've also noticed that when I removed serpents from Parkinson's patients, they experienced a marked improvement in their shaking and motor function.

It's worth noting that basal ganglia damage is also associated with attention deficit hyperactivity disorder (ADHD). ADHD often involves impaired dopamine neuron function, resulting in lower levels of dopamine in the brains of ADHD patients.[18] Dopamine is a key chemical (neurotransmitter) that brings feelings of peace, calm, and overall well-being. It helps us maintain a state of balance and rest. The basal ganglia contain high concentrations of dopamine.[19]

ACTIVATION

Let's proceed to judge this serpent that affects the basal ganglia in the name of Jesus. Are you ready? I'm here to guide you.

> *Father, in the name of Jesus, I address every serpentine spirit entwined around the basal ganglia—the reptilian brain—in myself and my loved one. (Insert the name of your loved one here.)*
>
> *In the powerful name of Jesus, I now pronounce judgment on the activities of this serpent. I release the holy fire emanating from the judicial bench of the Ancient of Days*

to expose this serpent, to force it out of its hidden recesses, and to consume the chaff that I have in common with this serpent right now. By the authority of Jesus' name I command the chaff within my soul or my loved one's soul to be utterly incinerated, and I command this malevolent serpent to vacate its position coiled around the basal gan-glia—the reptilian brain.

Now I declare the Lord's judgment on this wicked ser-pent, and I command it to depart. I take it up, as Jesus said I would do, and I unwind it from my brain stem by heavenly court order. I toss you into the consuming flames right now, in the name of Jesus! Burn and never return!

Now take Communion, and declare that the cross of Christ is crushing the head of this serpent. Speak to your brain and the basal ganglia therein. Command any poisonous venom to come out of it, in Jesus' name.

Then speak these words aloud:

I rebuke and cast away the conditions of Parkinson's, Huntington's, Alzheimer's, restless leg syndrome, insomnia, and ADHD. I command the spirit of infirmity to exit immediately, in the name of Jesus. I declare a miraculous re-creation of tissue and nerves—with released dopamine, perfect chemical and hormonal balances, restored brain neurons, and repaired electrical signals. I decree a cre-ative miracle is taking place within my brain right now, in Jesus' name! Amen.

Note: If any of these physical issues have been going on for a while, you may need to soak in fiery worship to totally drive this serpent out.

Just so you know, in this little book there is no way I can give a comprehensive, detailed list of afflictions these serpents can cause. This is why you must rely on the Holy Spirit to reveal to you any other attachments they might have in your life. Good hunting!

CHAPTER 11

COMMISSIONED TO BE
A SNAKE HUNTER

He said to them, "Go into all the world and preach the
gospel to every creature. He who believes and is baptized
will be saved; but he who does not believe will be con-
demned. And these signs will follow those who believe:
In My name they will cast out demons; they will speak
with new tongues; they will take up serpents; and if they
drink anything deadly, it will by no means hurt them;
they will lay hands on the sick, and they will recover."
—MARK 16:15–18, NKJV

THIS PASSAGE OF Scripture is called the Great Commission. It's a call to a planet-wide missions trip, collectively accomplished when the entire body heeds the words of Jesus. All those who choose to do so will have astonishing signs following wherever their feet dare to tread. They will cast out demons, speak

211

in new tongues, drink deadly things with no ill effect, lay hands on the infirm, see miracles, and, yes, even take up serpents.

This book was designed to turn you into a snake hunter. This mantle will grow in its manifestation and authority as you step out to practice the biblical precepts you have learned. Because of these scriptural truths, you will experience a steady increase to discern, see, target, then "take up" serpents—not only off yourself but also off other people.

Now that you have been de-snakified, you can receive the commissioning as a full-blown snake hunter so you can usher in deliverance and healing for other people.

PAUL, THE SNAKE HUNTER

Paul was healed of the scars of his trauma through the power of Communion and his deep commitment to partake of it regularly. This authorized him to shake off the deadly viper on the island of Malta and remain unharmed. Do you remember what the people of Malta thought of Paul after they witnessed him overcoming the viper's bite, which they knew always produced death? The Bible says they called him "a god" (Acts 28:6).

Then revival swept Malta! Once Paul was de-snakified, something massive shifted in the spirit realm. A commissioning was released on him to be a snake hunter and deliver all the sick, snake-infected people on the island. Revival spread through the population because one man demonstrated his authority over the serpent.

Revival hits when we become de-snakified and are commissioned as snake hunters. Then we can go into all the earth to take up serpents that are causing disease, destruction, and lack of every kind.

MOSES, THE ORIGINAL SNAKE HUNTER

Moses had a wild life story. He was born at a time in which Pharaoh decreed that all male Hebrew babies were to be killed. In a preemptive move to save her baby, Moses' mother, Jochebed, hid him in a woven basket coated with bitumen and pitch to make it watertight. Then she gently placed the basket along the bank of the Nile River. Miriam, Moses' sister, stayed close to watch what would happen.

By God's providence Pharaoh's daughter was bathing in the Nile that day, and she spotted the basket among the reeds. As her servants pulled it out of the water, Miriam ran to Pharaoh's daughter and offered to find a Hebrew woman to nurse the baby. Accordingly Moses was taken back to his mother, who took care of the child until he was weaned. He was then returned to Pharaoh's daughter to be raised in the royal household. She named him Moses because she had drawn him out of the water.

From there, Moses grew up in Pharaoh's household as a prince of Egypt. It is estimated that Moses lived in the palace with his mother (Pharaoh's daughter), Pharaoh, and the rest of the royal family for at least twenty-five years and possibly until he was close to forty.

This means that Moses, as a prince, likely had access to the best Egypt had to offer: an opulent palace, exquisite food, expensive clothing, and all the culture's entertainment, not to mention the respect and admiration of the Egyptian citizens.

When it came to education, Moses likely had the finest tutors available in all the nation. The Bible says, "Moses was learned in all the wisdom of the Egyptians, and was mighty in words and deeds" (Acts 7:22, NKJV). Moses would have been fully schooled in all necessary academic and military applications.[1]

A very important aspect of the education system in Egypt was learning about the pantheon of gods the people worshipped. Idolatry was the central focus of their belief system and daily life. There were many gods, each with its own realm of power, and they required specific sacrifices and rituals to be appeased. Because these gods were believed to be the power source behind abundant crops, favorable weather, fertility, wealth, and military might, the accurate worship of each of them was considered of high importance.

In his daily schooling, Prince Moses had to learn about them all, especially the reigning god of the house of Pharaoh himself:

Wadjet, the "goddess of serpents, the Nile Delta...and protector of Egyptian kings."[2] She was an idol worshipped primarily by the elite. Her job was "to guard the kings of Egypt and to protect them from their enemies." Wadjet took the shape of a cobra, "who would strike out at the king's enemies if he were threatened. In ancient Egypt, the cobra was a very powerful and prestigious animal, symbolizing royalty and sovereignty."[3]

The Bible indicates that Wadjet was the power source for Pharaoh at the time of Israel's deliverance. Exodus 4:3 describes this serpent as "the symbol of royal and divine power worn on the crown of the Pharaohs."

In other words, Pharaoh's crown proudly displayed the image of his guardian deity and power source. Moses, as a royal prince, was no doubt thoroughly educated on this serpent. He may have even made sacrifices to it at the instruction of his tutors and family. In fact he lived under the rule of that demonic serpent for decades before finally fleeing Egypt after killing an Egyptian who was beating an Israelite slave.

Was Moses left unaffected by this level of exposure to that evil snake? As you will see, just like Paul who carried around a deadly viper unawares, so Moses was prey to this serpent, which was a master of camouflage technology.

THE TREE OF FIRE

Fast-forward forty years. Moses had been living in the desert as a shepherd since his exile from Egypt. Then one fateful day he had an encounter with God on Mount Horeb that defined the rest of his life. Let's take a look:

> Now Moses kept the flock of Jethro his father-in-law, the
> priest of Midian; and he led the flock to the back or west
> side of the wilderness and came to Horeb or Sinai, the
> mountain of God. The Angel of the Lord appeared to
> him in a flame of fire out of the midst of a bush; and he

looked, and behold, the bush burned with fire, yet was
not consumed. And Moses said, I will now turn aside and
see this great sight, why the bush is not burned. And when
the Lord saw that he turned aside to see, God called to
him out of the midst of the bush and said, Moses, Moses!
And he said, Here am I. God said, Do not come near; put
your shoes off your feet, for the place on which you stand
is holy ground.

—EXODUS 3:1–5

Moses had lived in the desert for four decades and never witnessed a sight such as this. I'm sure he had seen many bushes catch
fire due to the lightning from frequent desert storms. However, this
tree, mind-bogglingly, was not being burned to a crisp.

As Moses turned aside to witness this phenomenon, to look
closer to see why the bush was not burning up, he came face to
face with God. What followed was God's commissioning of Moses
to free the Israelite nation from the jurisdiction of the snake king,
Pharaoh, and the nation of Egypt.

And the Lord said, I have surely seen the affliction of My
people who are in Egypt, and have heard their cry because
of their taskmasters and oppressors; for I know their sor-
rows and sufferings and trials. And I have come down to
deliver them out of the hand and power of the Egyptians
and to bring them up out of that land to a land good
and large, a land flowing with milk and honey [a land of
plenty]—to the place of the Canaanite, the Hittite, the
Amorite, the Perizzite, the Hivite, and the Jebusite. Now
behold, the cry of the Israelites has come to Me, and I
have also seen how the Egyptians oppress them. Come
now therefore, and I will send you to Pharaoh, that you
may bring forth My people, the Israelites, out of Egypt.

—EXODUS 3:7–10

Moses was being charged and commissioned to liberate God's
people from the control of Pharaoh, who literally wore a demonic

serpent on his crown. In essence this means that Moses was called to be a snake hunter.

Moses immediately responded to God's commissioning with arguments of his own inadequacies, saying things like "Who am I, that I should go to Pharaoh and bring the Israelites out of Egypt?" (v. 11). He added that the Israelite people "will not believe me or listen to and obey my voice; for they will say, The Lord has not appeared to you" (4:1). Moses even protested God's command to go and free the people by bringing up his speech impediment: "O Lord, I am not eloquent or a man of words, neither before nor since You have spoken to Your servant; for I am slow of speech and have a heavy and awkward tongue" (v. 10).

It's interesting to note that Moses, who had been raised in a palace and tutored by the world's best educators, was beset with so many fears and such a severe lack of confidence. What was really going on here? Could Moses' apprehension in facing Pharaoh be coming from a demonic presence he had in common with the snake king?

This is one of the main reasons God met Moses that day using the miraculous wonder of a tree that was on fire but didn't burn up. Let's look more closely at this astounding spectacle.

FIRE BURNS UP THE CHAFF AND DRIVES THE SERPENT OUT OF HIDING

Why would God set a tree on fire? We have to ask ourselves this question. The Father is very specific and intentional in every single move He makes. The God of all the universe doesn't just pull a miraculous sign out of a hat. Rather, He calculatingly assigns a particular wonder to a specific event to accomplish a kingdom objective.

The ten plagues were implemented not just to scare the pants off the Egyptians and cause them to release Israel from slavery. They were very specific judgments against the demonic gods of Egypt. The parting of the Red Sea not only enabled the Israelites to escape the Egyptians as their captors were drowned but also positioned the children of Israel to be "baptized" into Moses and the glory cloud (1 Cor. 10:2). When God stopped up the waters of the Jordan River, which backed up all the way to a city called Adam, He made a way for Israel to cross over into the Promised Land. But in addition, it symbolized our crossing over into our promised land through Christ and His cross, as well as the wiping clean of our sins—all the way back to the garden.

God is so precise. So, what was His intent that day on the mountain with the miraculous sign of the burning bush? God was calling a man, who would be likened to the Christ. He would be the one to free the people from the control of the snake king, just as Jesus would. And the only way for that man, Moses, to succeed in his mission was to have nothing in him left in common with the serpent that ruled Pharaoh's house.

That's why fire was used—not a rainbow, a glory cloud, or even a plague, but pure, raw, blazing fire that could not be quenched. Moses had chaff inside his soul that needed to be burned up by that fire. Plus, he had been carrying around a serpent for decades, one he had no clue existed. It could be driven out of its hiding place only by God's holy fire; thus, the tree stood blazing before Moses.

WHAT'S REALLY IN YOUR HAND?

Chapter 4 of the Book of Exodus starts with Moses protesting the call of God, all the while standing directly in front of the bush that was burning yet not consumed. Watch how this unfolds.

> And Moses answered, But behold, they will not believe me or listen to and obey my voice; for they will say, The Lord has not appeared to you. And the Lord said to him, What is that in your hand? And he said, A rod. And He said, Cast it on the ground. And he did so and it became a serpent [the symbol of royal and divine power worn on the crown of the Pharaohs]; and Moses fled from before it.
> —EXODUS 4:1–3

So, again, Moses started in with his doubts and insufficiencies. Nevertheless, notice God's response. He didn't address anything Moses said. In fact He appeared to just plain ignore it! Instead the Lord steered the conversation to the question He had been trying to get to: "What is that in your hand?" This is a strange inquiry from an omniscient God, who knows all. It wasn't that God didn't know what was in Moses' hand. He wanted to see if *Moses* recognized what he had been carrying around for over forty years!

Totally oblivious to reality, Moses ignorantly answered, "A rod." God then instructed him to throw it down right in front of the fiery bush. When Moses obeyed, the rod became what it actually had been the entire time: a demonic serpent.

Snakes are masters of camouflage technology. Moses had been walking around for forty years, carrying a serpent he likely had picked up in Pharaoh's house during his youth. Using the power of His fiery presence, God drove that demon out of its hiding place. Thus, Moses had an "apostle Paul" moment, with the fire exposing what had been in his hand all those years.

MOSES HAD CHAFF

The fire was also there to bring Moses healing from the chaff he had in common with that cobra. Notice the Bible says that when the rod became a serpent, Moses "fled from before it" (v. 3). Why did he run in fear? Moses had lived in the desert for forty years, during which time he must have encountered countless snakes. Those moments surely built up his confidence, so why would he be afraid of a serpent now?

When you have something in common with a demonic snake, you have no dominion over it. That's why Jesus said, "The prince (evil genius, ruler) of the world is coming....[He has nothing in common with Me...*and he has no power over Me*]" (John 14:30, emphasis added). The serpent has no power over you when there is nothing in you that belongs to it—no fear, doubt, or insecurities of any kind.

I believe Moses' lack of confidence in taking on Pharaoh was because they had something in common: the serpent that guarded the palace. Moses had lived under the cobra's rule for years. He likely had even been taught to worship and offer sacrifices to it!

Therefore, the second reason the tree of fire was necessary was to burn away the chaff—the briars and thorns, the wicked internal foe—in Moses' vineyard. Then that serpent in Pharaoh's house would not have power over him, and he could destroy it.

Let's consider the proof that Moses was healed in his soul while standing in the fiery presence of God. After he ran from the snake, the Father instructed him to do this:

> Put forth your hand and take it by the tail. And he stretched out his hand and caught it, and it became a rod in his hand.
>
> —Exodus 4:4

When I read that, I thought, "Seriously, God, no one in their right mind would pick up a snake by the tail! People who don't know better would experience the serpent whipping around to sink its deadly fangs into their flesh." Moses, being a longtime desert dweller, would have been quite aware of this fact. He must have also questioned God's instructions, yet he obeyed. The Bible says that when he stretched out and caught the snake's tail, "it became a rod in his hand."

Something supernatural happened within Moses as he stood in front of that fiery bush. He went from fleeing the serpent in fear to boldly laying hold of it. In the presence of the fire Moses was healed, his chaff burned to a crisp. He now possessed so much dominion over the serpent that even though he grabbed it by the tail, it could not bite him. Instead it turned into the real power rod of God! This was the very rod that would call down the plagues on Israel's captors, part the Red Sea for the nation's escape, strike the rock to bring forth water for millions in the desert, and defeat all their enemies along the route.

God had to meet Moses with fire on the mountain, for Moses was being commissioned to take out the snake king! He would have never succeeded if he'd still had something in common with the ruling power over Pharaoh's house. Because of this fiery encounter, Moses was fully equipped to undo Wadjet's jurisdiction over the nation of Israel. Later Moses' rod would even swallow up the serpents that Pharaoh's magicians wielded against him, as their rods transformed into living snakes.

WHAT ARE YOU CARRYING IN YOUR HAND?

It's disgusting that the snake had the nerve to disguise itself as a shepherd's rod in Moses' hand. It's just what a snake in the grass would do. Do you remember the woman with the spirit of divination we discussed earlier? She was speaking very godly sounding words, yet they were originating from the forked tongue of a python.

Likewise, I'll never forget what God told me while I was reading the story of Moses: "Many pastors are ruling their flock with a shepherd's rod that's really a serpent in disguise." Snakes love to invade the church masquerading as the things of God, working through what we say, what we teach, and how we act. Be careful what rod you use to guide your sheep. If you don't get de-snakified, your position of authority could infect your flock with toxic serpents and their venom.

Even the most gifted believer can be carrying a serpent. I recall listening to a very famous pastor who taught powerful sermons containing incredible biblical insights. Over the course of several weeks, though, I started noticing that he would chastise his team severely from the stage while preaching. They weren't moving fast enough, or they had committed some sort of infraction that upset him. Honestly, it bothered me. But I know that no person is perfect, so I continued to eat the meat and spit out the bones.

However, one day while tuning in, I experienced something very concerning. I was wearing my wired headphones while watching on my device. Suddenly the pastor went off on his staff again. That is when I saw two black serpents zipping up the wires of my headset. Furiously I jerked them out of my ears as fast as I could, narrowly avoiding a demonic implantation of the deaf adder that stops the ear.

I still think that pastor has amazing revelation from God. Yet he—like all of us—needs to repent of pride and the venom of asps that is under his lips. Then he needs to soak in the fire to get de-snakified.

I don't share this story to make you afraid. However, wisdom dictates that if you see or hear something that concerns you, such as the behavior I witnessed, ask God to reveal to you whether it has snakes on it. Also, don't judge that person; instead, release fire from heaven on them to drive out the serpents where they can see them, and ask the heavenly court to judge those demonic snakes on their behalf.

SNAKES IN YOUR GIFT BAG

Years ago, when I first received these revelations about serpents, God gave me a vision. I was walking around a park, gift bag in hand. In the vision I felt so proud of my gifts. But then, all of a sudden, I heard the rattling of a snake's tail, and then I sensed the movement of a serpent in my bag. Quickly setting the bag down, I moved away from it, shouting, "Everybody, step back!" Sure enough, out slithered a huge serpent. Thankfully, it departed from us, leaving everyone behind safe and sound.

Obviously God was showing me that I had snakes attached to my gifts that could infect the people to whom I was ministering. It's no coincidence that at the time of this vision, I had been soaking in a lot of fire. It drove that snake out of my bag, just like it drove the serpent off the rod of Moses. I encourage anyone in ministry or business to immerse yourself in fire; otherwise you could be releasing snakes into the area of influence in which God has placed you.

THE SERPENT IS ASTUTE

You have to be aware that the serpent is astute. He's going to try to get you off course from the true calling and commission God has on your life. Consider this verse:

> Now the serpent was *more astute* than all the animals of the field which the LORD God had made. And he said unto the woman, Has God indeed said, Ye shall not eat of every tree of the garden?
> —GENESIS 3:1, JUB, EMPHASIS ADDED

The word *astute* means "having or showing an ability to accurately assess situations or people and turn this to one's advantage."[4] Satan, that old serpent, is able to accurately assess a situation and turn it to his advantage. He sees the breaks in your hedge that consist of unholy desires, which give him the ability to drive you off course, then cause you to eat from the wrong tree.

I once knew a man who worked for an apostle of a high-level ministry. Though warfare was coming against the ministry as a whole, God was positioning this man to increase as the ministry did likewise. However, pride and ambition got the best of him. Thinking the grass was greener on the other side, he left his position, fueled by what he claimed was "God's voice" guiding him. Well, he didn't realize the snake speaks too! Soon he discovered that there were snakes in that grass and that they were squeezing out every opportunity connected to the platforms he thought were available to him. To this day he has been unemployed and left stripped, naked, and beaten by the serpent, much like Paul was in the marketplace, for all to see.

Watch out for the unsanctified desires in your soul. In the garden the serpent spoke to Eve, twisting God's word to deceive her into eating from the wrong tree. Look at this verse, and you will see that the unhealthy desires in Eve's soul brought about her downfall:

> When the woman saw that the tree was good (suitable, pleasant) for food and that it was delightful to look at, and a tree to be desired in order to make one wise, she took of its fruit and ate; and she gave some also to her husband, and he ate.
>
> —Genesis 3:6

She "saw" the tree was good and desirable, even though God had said not to eat of it. The eyes are the windows to the soul. Thus, it was the soulish yearnings in her inner being that enabled the snake to drive her to eat from the wrong tree.

The serpent is astute. He sees what cravings you have in your heart. He will then speak lies into your mind and present you with "opportunities" he knows will tempt those unsanctified areas in your nature. That's why you must keep your heart clean and burning with fire so that the most astute beast of the field will not be able to drive you out of your own garden.

Being De-snakified Brings a Wealth Transfer

Let's return to chapter 3 of the Book of Exodus, where God was commissioning Moses to free His people from the slavery of Egypt and the control of the snake king. As God laid out the Israelites' escape mission to Moses, He ended the chapter by saying:

> And I will give this people favor and respect in the sight of the Egyptians; and it shall be that when you go, you shall not go empty-handed. But every woman shall [insistently] solicit of her neighbor and of her that may be residing at her house jewels and articles of silver and gold, and garments,

which you shall put on your sons and daughters; and you
shall strip the Egyptians [of belongings due to you].
                                            —EXODUS 3:21–22

Here, God gave His children instructions to plunder Egypt
as they departed. In the Bible, Egypt often represents the world.
The same serpent spirit that ruled Pharaoh and Egypt is currently
wrapped around the leaders and the people of the world today.
There is a wealth transfer that happens when you become de-
snakified! It's no coincidence that in the very next chapter Moses
was freed of the snake that he had in common with the system of
Egypt. Thus, when the time came to leave the land, God's word of
a wealth transfer fully came to pass. The serpent's power could no
longer stop it.

> The Israelites did according to the word of Moses; and
> they [urgently] asked of the Egyptians jewels of silver
> and of gold, and clothing. The Lord gave the people
> favor in the sight of the Egyptians, so that they gave
> them what they asked. And they stripped the Egyptians
> [of those things].
>   —EXODUS 12:35–36

Once you have shaken off that snake, you can solicit Egypt to
hand over its wealth, and it will give you whatever you ask! God
will make the world favorably disposed toward you, just like He
did for the Israelites! This wealth transfer will enable the entire
body of Christ to escape the world's financial system, a structure
that has kept the church broke. The world does not take the body
of Christ seriously, which forces us to get our funding from other
believers. However, to operate in the highest realm of prosperity,
we must tap in to the deep pockets of the world—both its leaders
and its population.

I prophetically believe that we are entering a new era of fiscal
freedom for the church as a whole. God has already given us the
power to create wealth (Deut. 8:18), but in this new season He is

breathing on the businesses and creations of believers like never before. This includes the Father releasing downloads of wisdom, opening supernatural doors of favor and opportunity, providing start-up money for businesses, giving direction for explosive investment strategies, and much more. Now, along with this corporate deliverance from the python, which has squeezed out our gains, and our newfound dominion over the Egyptian snakes of the world, the resistance to a full manifestation of the wealth transfer is being removed.

ACTIVATION

You're like Moses. You've been walking around carrying a snake, and you didn't even know it. To walk out your God-given commission, you must first soak in fire.

Soak in fire to drive it out. Soak in fire to burn up the chaff. You've got to force that serpent out of your gift bag. Repent for any times you might have shepherded people with a rod that was really a serpent. Also repent for any time when you had serpents mixed in with your gifts and were releasing those serpents on people instead of getting them healed.

Do an elongated fire soak, and ask God to release a new baptism of fire on you to burn away your chaff and drive the serpents out of hiding.

I challenge you to spend an hour in fiery worship each day for the next week. Be like Moses, and turn aside to encounter this tree on fire!

Take some time now, if you can, to pray in fiery tongues as you listen to "Fire of God" by Mercy Culture.[5] Decree that the wealth transfer is coming because you have been de-snakified from the serpents of Egypt.

Now enter the heavenly court for the following activation.

Father, I ascend up the mountain, like Moses did, where the burning tree of fire is located. It's the fire of God that

*is in the court of the Ancient of Days! The wheels of fire
on the judge's bench are going back in time to where the
serpent entered my life in the first place, and streams of
fire are coming out from the judge's bench to burn my soul
with fire, exposing and driving out that slippery snake. I
thank You, Father, right now for Your mercy. I go into
court, submitting my call and every gift that I have. I
submit my shepherd's rod to You to burn it with fire, to
drive out any serpents that have anything in common with
my call or are intertwined with my gifts.*

*If I've been carrying around any serpent that has been
stealing power from my rod of authority, I judge it now.
Or if I have been beating the flock over the head with
a serpent instead of guiding them with a shepherd's rod,
then I repent. Drive it out now with holy fire, Lord.*

*Holy fire, holy fire! Bring me into that mountaintop
encounter, Lord, in front of the tree that burns with fire
but never burns up. Bring me to that place, Your fiery
presence.*

*I ask You for all-consuming fire. I call now for that
unquenchable fire, God, that nothing can put out. No
demonic serpent can put it out. No demonic strategy can
put it out. No attitude problem can put it out. No situation can put it out. No trauma can put it out. It's the
unquenchable, unstoppable fire of God.*

*Lord, I ask You to call forth the angels that are like
winds of fire to stand over me while I sleep and to cause
me to burn with fire. Have Your angels burn in the
churches today to clear them of serpents; burn in Your
children's businesses to remove all serpentine activity. And
ignite the fiery passion in me to drive out any snakes from
my gifts, callings, mandates, and visions right now.*

*As the fire burns within me, I know Your Word says we
will be baptized with the Holy Spirit and with fire. Baptize me now—right now—God. Fill me with fire and*

Your power, and cause me, Lord, to be cleaned of every bit of chaff, every bit of wickedness, every internal foe, every briar, every thorn, in the name of Jesus, so that I can grab the rod of power and deliver Your people, Lord. I declare that I am completely de-snakified and becoming Your snake hunter, Lord, in Jesus' name.

Lord, I ask You for the holy commissioning that You imparted to Moses on the mountain right now, as I stand before You in front of Your burning bush. Father, I ask You to drive that serpent out of hiding so I can be commissioned by You and, by heaven, to go forth and deliver Your people in great masses, my God. I throw my shepherd's rod down at Your fiery feet. As it manifests what it really has been this whole time—a serpent disguising itself as a rod of power—I will pick it up unafraid, because I have been healed of everything I had in common with it. Now I will wield the real rod of power to lead Your people out of slavery into freedom in Christ.

I receive Jesus' commission from Mark 16. I will go forth and preach the gospel, baptize the nations in the name of Jesus, drive out demons, heal the sick, and even take up serpents. I receive the mantle of commissioning to be a snake hunter right now, in the name of Jesus. I decree that my eyes will open; I will see the serpents on people, and I will take them up as Jesus declared. As I walk with this anointed rod, the staff of God, it will swallow up every demonic serpent that comes to oppress Your people, Lord.

Now take the rod in your hand, and as a prophetic act, throw it on the ground and judge that serpent. Command it to come out, in the name of Jesus. Then reach down and grab your new rod of power and use it to go forth and deliver the nations of the affliction and control of the snake king.

Don't let demonic serpents wreak havoc on your health, mental and emotional wellness, finances, and relationships. God has given us victory over all the power of the enemy, so let's walk in it!

If you've been delivered after reading this book, or if you hear or experience testimonies of other people who got delivered, please let me know. When you have a dream about serpents, when you see a vision of a serpent and pull it off yourself or someone else, or when you or someone else receives a miracle, send me the testimony. Email me a video or written testimony at selfies@katiesouza.com, and we might share your miracle on our show.

NOTES

CHAPTER 1

1. Blue Letter Bible, s.v. *"adikeō,"* accessed April 19, 2024, https://www.blueletterbible.org/lexicon/g91/nkjv/tr/0-1/.
2. Blue Letter Bible, s.v. *"airō,"* accessed April 19, 2024, https://www.blueletterbible.org/lexicon/g142/nkjv/tr/0-1/.

CHAPTER 2

1. Mark DeJesus, "10 Signs You Have a Religious Spirit," Turning Hearts Ministries International, September 22, 2017, https://markdejesus.com/10-signs-religious-spirit/.
2. Blue Letter Bible, s.v. *"pythōn,"* accessed April 22, 2024, https://www.blueletterbible.org/lexicon/g4436/kjv/tr/0-1/.
3. Blue Letter Bible, s.v. *"pythōn."*

CHAPTER 3

1. Amy Woodyatt, "Gigantic New Snake Species Discovered in Amazon Rainforest," CNN, updated February 23, 2024, https://www.cnn.com/2024/02/23/americas/worlds-biggest-snake-amazon-intl-scli-scn/index.html.
2. Blue Letter Bible, s.v. *"plēthos,"* accessed April 24, 2024, https://www.blueletterbible.org/lexicon/g4128/esv/mgnt/0-1/.
3. Patrick May, "So What Is It With Snakes and Wildfires?," *The Mercury News*, August 1, 2018, https://web.archive.org/web/20180803094801/https://www.mercurynews.com/2018/08/01/so-what-is-it-with-snakes-and-wildfires/.

4. Katie Souza, *The Serpent and the Soul Fire Soak*, KatieSouza.
com, accessed April 24, 2024, https://katiesouza.com/product/the-
serpent-and-soul-fire-soak/.

5. Blue Letter Bible, s.v. *"exousia,"* accessed April 24, 2024, https://
www.blueletterbible.org/lexicon/g1849/esv/mgnt/0-1/.

6. Blue Letter Bible, s.v. *"adikeō."*

7. I suggest Worship Forever, "Fire of God / 3 Hour Worship / Mercy
Culture Worship," YouTube, March 16, 2023, https://www.youtube.
com/watch?v=Yr066E55n7E.

CHAPTER 4

1. Susan Scutti, "A Brief History of Antivenom," *Global Health
Matters 21*, no. 5 (September/October 2022): 6, https://www.fic.
nih.gov/News/GlobalHealthMatters/september-october-2022/Pages/
antivenom-brief-history.aspx.

2. *The New Oxford Dictionary of English*, s.v. "hostile," 2001, https://
archive.org/details/newoxforddiction0000unse_g1s3/page/886/mode
/2up?view=theater&q=hostile.

3. *The New Oxford Dictionary of English*, s.v. "discharge," 2001,
https://archive.org/details/newoxforddiction0000unse_g1s3/
page/524/mode/2up?view=theater&q=discharge.

4. "There Is No Spoon—The Matrix (5/9) Movie Clip (1999),"
Movieclips, YouTube, May 26, 2011, https://www.youtube.com/
watch?v=XO0pcWxcROI.

5. Blue Letter Bible, s.v. *"sōzō,"* accessed April 29, 2024, https://www.
blueletterbible.org/lexicon/g4982/esv/mgnt/0-1/.

6. *Merriam-Webster*, s.v. "opposition," accessed June 17, 2024, https://
www.merriam-webster.com/dictionary/opposition; *The New Oxford
Dictionary of English*, s.v. "opposition," 2001, https://archive.org/
details/newoxforddiction0000unse_g1s3/page/1302/mode/2up?view
=theater&q=opposition.

7. Blue Letter Bible, s.v. *"thronos,"* accessed April 29, 2024, https://
www.blueletterbible.org/lexicon/g2362/esv/mgnt/0-1/.

8. *The New Oxford Dictionary of English*, s.v. "discharge."

CHAPTER 5

1. Blue Letter Bible, s.v. *"pinō,"* accessed April 30, 2024, https://www.
blueletterbible.org/lexicon/g4095/esv/mgnt/0-1/.

2. Blue Letter Bible, s.v. "*dipsaō*," accessed April 30, 2024, https:// www.blueletterbible.org/lexicon/g1372/esv/mgnt/0-1/.

3. Blue Letter Bible, s.v. "*astheneia*," accessed May 1, 2024, https:// www.blueletterbible.org/lexicon/g769/kjv/tr/0-1/.

4. Blue Letter Bible, s.v. "*klaō*," accessed May 1, 2024, https://www. blueletterbible.org/lexicon/g2806/esv/mgnt/0-1/.

5. Blue Letter Bible, s.v. "*artos*," accessed May 1, 2024, https://www. blueletterbible.org/lexicon/g740/esv/mgnt/0-1/.

CHAPTER 6

1. Blue Letter Bible, s.v. "*livyātān*," accessed May 1, 2024, https:// www.blueletterbible.org/lexicon/h3882/esv/wlc/0-1/.

2. Make sure that throughout this study, you soak in my brand-new *The Serpent and the Soul Fire Soak*, which you can find at katiesouza.com/product/the-serpent-and-soul-fire-soak/.

CHAPTER 7

1. BioBeats, "How Unprocessed Trauma Is Stored in the Body," Medium, January 21, 2020, https://medium.com/@biobeats/how-unprocessed-trauma-is-stored-in-the-body-10222a76cbad.

2. Please watch my teaching "Matter Holds Memory" on my YouTube channel at www.youtube.com/watch?v=M7KeymPLoAs. Then obtain and listen to my *Sons of the Light Teach and Soak Combo* (available at katiesouza.com/product/sons-of-light-bundle/) to drive these memories out of your physical body. If you don't, they could lead to severe sickness and even eventual death.

3. *The New Oxford Dictionary of English*, s.v. "fetter," 2001, https:// archive.org/details/newoxforddiction0000unse_g1s3/page/676/ mode/2up?view=theater&q=fetter.

4. Blue Letter Bible, s.v. "*exousia*."

5. Blue Letter Bible, s.v. "*exousia*."

6. Blue Letter Bible, s.v. "*adikeō*."

7. Blue Letter Bible, s.v. "*bāriah*," accessed May 2, 2024, https://www. blueletterbible.org/lexicon/h1281/nkjv/wlc/0-1/.

Chapter 8

1. *The New Oxford Dictionary of English*, s.v. "divination," 2010, https://archive.org/details/newoxforddiction0000unse_g1s3/page/538/mode/2up?view=theater&q=divination.
2. Blue Letter Bible, s.v. "*pythōn*."
3. Blue Letter Bible, s.v. "*apantaō*," accessed May 3, 2024, https://www.blueletterbible.org/lexicon/g528/kjv/tr/0-1/.
4. Blue Letter Bible, s.v. "*pythōn*."
5. *The New Oxford Dictionary of English*, s.v. "ventriloquist," 2001, https://archive.org/details/newoxforddiction0000unse_g1s3/page/2052/mode/2up?view=theater&q=ventriloquist.
6. Dr. Francis Myles, in communication with the author.

Chapter 9

1. Blue Letter Bible, s.v. "*alalos*," accessed May 4, 2024, https://www.blueletterbible.org/lexicon/g216/kjv/tr/0-1/.
2. Blue Letter Bible, s.v. "*Timaios*," accessed May 4, 2024, https://www.blueletterbible.org/lexicon/g5090/kjv/tr/0-1/; Blue Letter Bible, s.v. "*ṭāmē'* (adj.)" accessed May 4, 2024, https://www.blueletterbible.org/lexicon/h2931/kjv/wlc/0-1/.
3. Blue Letter Bible, s.v. "*ṭāmē'* (v.)," accessed May 4, 2024, https://www.blueletterbible.org/lexicon/h2930/kjv/wlc/0-1/.
4. Blue Letter Bible, s.v. "*airō*."
5. Marquez Collins, in communication with the author.
6. Marquez Collins, in communication with the author.
7. Blue Letter Bible, s.v. "*ṭᵊhôrîm*, accessed May 6, 2024, https://www.blueletterbible.org/lexicon/h2914/kjv/wlc/0-1/.
8. Ralph Holliday, in communication with the author.

Chapter 10

1. Mary H. Dyer, "Common Mandrake Uses—What Is Mandrake Used For," Gardening Know How, last updated February 1, 2023, https://www.gardeningknowhow.com/ornamental/flowers/mandrake/common-mandrake-uses.htm.
2. Adam Eliyahu Berkowitz, "25 Mysterious Fires at Food Processing Plants Across US; 'End-of-Days Food Shortage,'" Israel365 News, May 2, 2022, https://www.thehouseofdavid.org/prophetic-map/2022/5/3/25-mysterious-fires-at-food-processing-plants-across-us-end-of-days-food-shortage; Grant Miller, "North American Plant

and Factory Disasters in 2023," My Patriot Supply, April 27, 2023, https://www.mypatriotsupply.com/blogs/scout/north-american-plant-and-factory-disasters-in-2023.

3. Joanna Thompson, "Lab Grown Meat Approved for Sale: What You Need to Know," *Scientific American*, June 30, 2023, https://www.scientificamerican.com/article/lab-grown-meat-approved-for-sale-what-you-need-to-know/.

4. "Lab-Grown Meat: 53 Hazards Identified by FAO-WHO," European Livestock Voice, April 24, 2023, https://meatthefacts.eu/home/activity/beyond-the-headlines/lab-grown-meat-53-hazards-identified-by-fao-who/.

5. "5 Reasons Why Eating Insects Could Reduce Climate Change," World Economic Forum, February 9, 2022, https://www.weforum.org/agenda/2022/02/how-insects-positively-impact-climate-change/

6. "Leading Causes of Death," Centers for Disease Control and Prevention, last reviewed May 2, 2024, https://www.cdc.gov/nchs/fastats/leading-causes-of-death.htm.

7. Melissa M. Lane et al., "Ultra-Processed Food Exposure and Adverse Health Outcomes: Umbrella Review of Epidemiological Meta-Analyses," *The BMJ* 384, no. 8419 (February 28, 2024), https://doi.org/10.1136/bmj-2023-077310.

8. Euridice Martinez Steele et al., "Ultra-processed Foods and Added Sugars in the US Diet: Evidence from a Nationally Representative Cross-sectional Study," *BMJ Open* 6, no. 3 (2016), https://www.ncbi.nlm.nih.gov/pmc/articles/PMC4785287/.

9. Karen Kaplan, "What's Wrong With the U.S. Diet? More Than Half Our Calories From 'Ultra-Processed' Food," *Orlando Sentinel*, March 14, 2016, https://www.orlandosentinel.com/2016/03/14/whats-wrong-with-the-us-diet-more-than-half-our-calories-from-ultra-processed-food/.

10. Bible Tools, s.v. "*nephesh*," accessed May 6, 2024, https://www.bibletools.org/index.cfm/fuseaction/lexicon.show/id/h5315/nephesh.htm.

11. Blue Letter Bible, s.v., "*dipsaō*."

12. Blue Letter Bible, s.v., "*peinaō*," accessed May 7, 2024, https://www.blueletterbible.org/lexicon/g3983/kjv/tr/0-1/.

13. Mayo Clinic Staff, "Gout," Mayo Clinic, November 16, 2022, https://www.mayoclinic.org/diseases-conditions/gout/symptoms-causes/syc-20372897.

14. Mayo Clinic Staff, "Gout."

15. Mayo Clinic Staff, "Gout."

16. Cecile Beatson, "Yellow-bellied Sea Snake," Australian Museum, November 19, 2020, https://australian.museum/learn/animals/reptiles/yellow-bellied-sea-snake/#.

17. "Our Three Brains—The Reptilian Brain," Interaction Design Foundation, accessed May 7, 2024, https://www.interaction-design.org/literature/article/our-three-brains-the-reptilian-brain.

18. Martyn Bryson, "What's the Relationship Between ADHD and Dopamine?," Psycom, updated May 1, 2023, https://www.psycom.net/adhd/adhd-and-dopamine.

19. Karen S. Rommelfanger and Thomas Wichmann, "Extrastriatal Dopaminergic Circuits of the Basal Ganglia," *Frontiers in Neuroanatomy* 4, no. 139 (October 27, 2010), https://www.ncbi.nlm.nih.gov/pmc/articles/PMC2987554/.

Chapter 11

1. Dewey M. Beegle, "Moses," Encyclopaedia Britannica, April 23, 2024, https://www.britannica.com/biography/Moses-Hebrew-prophet/Years-and-deeds.

2. Joseph Comunale, "Wadjet in Egyptian Mythology / Symbols, Depiction, and Origins: Frequently Asked Questions," Study.com, updated January 9, 2023, https://study.com/academy/lesson/wadjet-symbol-facts-overview-snake-egyptian-goddess.html.

3. "Wadjet," Odyssey Online, Michael C. Carlos Museum of Emory University, accessed May 7, 2024, https://carlos.emory.edu/htdocs/ODYSSEY/EGYPT/Wadjet.html.

4. *The New Oxford Dictionary of English*, s.v. "astute," 2010, https://archive.org/details/newoxforddiction0000unse_g1s3/page/104/mode/2up?view=theater&q=astute.

5. Worship Forever, "Fire of God / 3 Hour Worship / Mercy Culture Worship," YouTube, March 16, 2023, https://www.youtube.com/watch?v=Yr066E55n7E.

ABOUT THE AUTHOR

KATIE SOUZA WAS a thug. She was a debt collector for multiple drug dealers, the "enforcer" who went to collect on those who owed her dealers money. She was afraid of nothing and no one and has been beaten, shot at, chased, and jailed multiple times.

Katie's life consisted of drugs, clandestine laboratories, stolen vehicles, high-speed chases, gun shoot-outs, and many arrests. She was one of the best meth cookers around, with people seeking her product. She was the black leather jacket-wearing biker who went where many feared to go. But when she was captured by federal marshals in February 1999, she was at the end of her rope. Charged with manufacturing, conspiracy, and gun possession, Katie was sentenced to twelve and a half years in a federal prison.

The pressures of her circumstances and the consequences of her previous lifestyle finally drove her into the arms of God. And the one who had been just a thug became a supernatural thug for Jesus! God used for His glory the same tenacity and fearlessness she had working for the devil. The Holy Spirit gave her a hunger for the Word. Soon after, she started a Bible study within her cellblock. Then one night God told Katie she would have a new release date. She fearlessly announced it to everyone. Despite the laughter and ridicule, Katie stood by the word she heard from the Lord, and eighteen months later His word came to pass the exact day God told her. Seven years were miraculously taken off her sentence, and she hasn't looked back. The Katie Souza you see today is the personification of the miracle God can perform in a yielded life.

Katie's first book was written while she was in prison. *The Key to Your Expected End* (The Captivity Series) has been in huge demand by inmates around the world since its release. In late 2006 the Lord released a healing anointing upon Katie. Since then, countless people have received miracles through her conferences and teaching resources. Katie has served more than four thousand prisons around the world with her resources and miracle meetings.

The Lord put a mandate on Katie to bring healing to His people through international media. In 2013, Katie and her staff began producing a television show called *Healing the Wounded Soul* and now produce *Faith With Katie*, which can be seen around the globe on major networks, including Channel 379 on DirecTV, and viewed on her website, katiesouza.com. She is part owner of Faith TV. Her live teachings and miracle services can also be seen on the Katie Souza Facebook page and YouTube channel.

She and her husband, Robert, are living out their expected end in Florida.